Rising out of the throes of [illegible] Hathaway has focused on [illegible] book, he offers a powerful challenge which will be as a welcomed rope tossed to the many who want to be rescued from the frantic "scrambling…for acceptance, success, and love." For a person who has either known the need to be rescued, or who lives in the role of the rescuer, I believe this is a remarkable resource.

Adrian B. Shepard
Retired Pastor/Church Administrator

Rick Hathaway is a man with a message, and in every setting that I've been honored to hear him speak, he has always illuminated the light of Christ. Rick is real, and his book has done a marvelous job of revealing to us real values. We live in a spiritually contentious culture, and his book throws out a lifeline to a de-sensitized Christian community. I wish that a book like this was around when I started in ministry twenty-six years ago.

Rev. Raymond Faircloth, Sr.
Senior Pastor of The Life Center

"Rick Hathaway's book, *A Legacy of Faith,* articulates so well the answer to all the deep issues of life that God wants everyone to know. You can read it in the book and allow it to change you, or you can learn the hard way… . Rick Hathaway is a wordsmith and he has wisdom from God to share. Are you tired of wearing a mask? Tired of disappointment, 'reaching for limbs that are just slightly out of reach'? Let God speak to you through this book and pull you up to higher ground!

Michelle Walters
FPHC of Saint Pauls, N.C.

a legacy of
faith

a fresh look at
blessing, morality,
self-worth, and mentorship

a legacy of
faith

Rick Hathaway

Tate Publishing & *Enterprises*

TATE PUBLISHING
& Enterprises

Published by Tate Publishing & Enterprises, LLC
127 E. Trade Center Terrace | Mustang, Oklahoma 73064 USA
1.888.361.9473 | www.tatepublishing.com

Tate Publishing is committed to excellence in the publishing industry. The company reflects the philosophy established by the founders, based on Psalms 68:11,
"The Lord gave the word and great was the company of those who published it."

Book design copyright © 2007 by Tate Publishing, LLC. All rights reserved.
Cover design by Janae Glass
Interior design by Jennifer Redden

Published in the United States of America

ISBN: 978-1-6024727-7-8
07.04.11

Acknowledgments

This book was initially intended to introduce my children to a grandfather they had never known. My oldest son was two when my father died. He had little time to sit on his lap and take walks up and down the street. Even more importantly, my children never had the immediate influence of his character in their lives. And so it was a few months back, contemplating my older years and remembering my father, that I decided to write this account as a formal thank you to him. His wonderful life and spiritual guidance is the first acknowledgment I offer.

Sometimes an acknowledgment needs to document an act of thank you as well. My wife has painstakingly walked this walk with me. She has seen my failings, been at the other end of my tirades, and on occasion held my hands to the anvil. She too deserves a very special thank you and acknowledgment of her value to me.

It is, therefore, in love, respect, and honor that I acknowledge my indebtedness to both of them with this thank you of appreciation.

For being fighters from the core, and warriors mentally and spiritually
I thank you
For standing up for right, the underprivileged, and the oppressed
I thank you
For your faithfulness to your families and your God
I thank you
For strong convictions of selfless surrender
I thank you
For your precious love of God and man
I thank you
For enduring pain and longsuffering
I thank you
For wisdom and counsel
I thank you
For quiet humility
I thank you

Table of Contents

Section #3: The Third Lie—"Life Has No Value"

Section #4: The Fourth Lie—"Males Are Meaningless"

Foreword

Understanding biblical principles with a democratic mindset can be somewhat difficult. It seems that if we hear a lie long enough and by enough people, it must be truth. But truth cannot be voted in by popular opinion.

This book will challenge you to look at areas of your life and possibly reconsider things you have been taught in the past. Some of the topics or lies covered in this book have been perpetuated by the media, by our western culture, and even by Christendom. (It's amazing to see the statistics on the percentage of Christians that do not have a biblical worldview). After reading the *A Legacy of Faith* you may have to put a sacred cow or two out to pasture. I pray that as you read Rick's writings, you will keep an open mind and have a teachable heart. Let the Holy Spirit guide you in all truth.

I recommend this book for both personal growth and as a small group study. These truths are for everyone. You will be blessed by Rick's personal stories as he takes a fresh look at blessing, morality, self-worth, and mentorship. Don't just read the book for inspiration, take it a step further and strive for transformation.

I have a question that I ask at times concerning people I come across on a daily basis. The question is, "Paycheck or passion?" The root of the question lies in whether a person does what they do out of a passion or merely for a paycheck. (I'm sure you've come across people that you wonder about)? Well I can vouch for both Rick and his wife Deborah and tell you that these two are as real as they come, and they do what they do out of passion. This passion stems from a love for God and love for people. It's not everyday that you meet someone like Rick Hathaway. I am blessed to call him my friend. After reading this book, I bet that you will feel like you know him too.

Dr. Jeffrey Hoglen, D.Min, D.CM
Founder: Open Arms International Ministries @ www.oaim.net
Author: Here Am I, the Call to Biblical Missions

Introduction

I was twelve, and my brother was sixteen. It was the middle of winter. We had just finished taking off our skates and putting on our shoes on the bank of a favorite ice skating pond nearby where we lived. A car drove up, and I noticed Tommy, a neighborhood boy, get out. He and I were about the same age and often hung out together.

He put on his skates and went out onto the ice. He had a new pair of skates, and was breaking them in on his first time out on the pond. Those of us who skated there often knew the pond's idiosyncrasies. We knew there was a dangerous current of water that flowed out from under a bridge nearby the embankment Tommy was skating around. In deep winter, a thin layer of ice would film over the flow of water, hiding the danger from unsuspecting skaters.

Tommy was skating too close to the current. We tried getting his attention by screaming out his name, and waving him away from the killer flow of water. But, he couldn't understand us and it was too late. With a sickening sound of broken ice we witnessed him plunge into the frigid water beneath him. Clinging desperately for life on the side of his icy tomb, he fought to keep from being swept away by the current that was pulling at him to surrender his grip and finalize the ultimate fate before him. Screams of terror filled the cold air as both Tommy and his mother, who had witnessed all this from the bank, were pleading for someone to pluck him out of the hands of the grim reaper.

My brother acted in heroic fashion. Grabbing a hockey stick, he and a friend darted across the ice toward the gaping hole where Tommy had moments ago been skating. My brother shouted instructions to his friend as both positioned themselves flat on the ice, nearing the death chamber.

I can still feel the terror I felt that morning. I knew someone had to reach Tommy quickly, but I also feared for the safety of my brother and his friend. Crawling closer and closer to the edge where Tommy had plunged, my brother and his friend were on way too thin ice. The ice was giving out cracks of warning as the two boys defiantly pressed forward anyway. Within just a few feet of where Tommy had just plummeted through the ice, my brother stretched out the hockey stick in his hand. That was the chain of survival! Tommy, holding on to the hockey stick in my brothers strong arms, while my brother's friend was holding my brother's feet. Little by little, they squirmed their way back onto solid ice, where they stood to their feet, and Tommy ran to his mother for comfort, warmth, and an eventual change of clothes.

Maybe you've been there, skating on thin ice, discouraged, angry with God, and ready to throw in the towel. My wife and I were walking up to the golf course nearby where we lived in Northern Vermont. I was just hoping that some of the brisk Fall air would breathe new life into my brain. As we strolled hand in hand, she listened patiently to my barrage of complaints against God, the church I was with, and the world! She whispered something gently to me that rattled inside my mind. It was a simple question really, "Why don't you quit and do something else for awhile?"

I searched in my heart for an answer that came literally from above. I looked up into the tall pines that were lining either side of the road. I imagined a little child having climbed up into one, only to find he was unable to get back down. Tottering dangerously in the tiny branches being swayed by the wind, he was crying for help. What would I do? What would you do? The urgency of the situation I had imagined caused me to remember why I do what I do. As Jeremiah said: "… his word is in my heart like a fire, a fire shut up in my bones. I am weary of holding it in; indeed, I cannot." (Jer 20:9 NIV).

We live in a country where people are tottering perilously in the trees of life. They are blown around dangerously by the winds of a great storm of lies. The lies affect Christian, non-Christian, agnostic, and atheist. They know no barriers, and are influencing both the rich and poor, targeting us all, regardless of ethnicity, age, or gender.

The lies have invaded our politics, our theology, our spiritual health, and our mental health. The lies are born out of a corrupted belief system that has influenced what we have come to believe about the blessing of God, morality, the value of life, and the purpose of gender.

I was born April 22, 1949. That puts me at the age of 56 at the time of this writing. The only reason I note that is to justify what I'm about to say. Age increases one's appreciation of the world around them, whether that's where they are going, or where they have been. In my case, I have learned through the years to appreciate my past, specifically those things handed down to me from my father.

My father has become my posthumous mentor. As I have reflected on his life through the years, I have remembered the example he laid before me. It has helped me keep on a decent path, and to recognize the lies in the world around me. Because of that, it is his example that I often refer to in this book.

It is with the same urgency that my brother and his friend ran to save Tommy, and, with the same conviction that Jeremiah had to release the "fire shut up in his bones," that I write this book. With that passion I hope to stimulate the readers thinking.

The screaming of God's angels can practically be heard in the heavens, and I'm sounding a warning cry. As a nation, we are skating on thin ice. I have a lifeline to throw, a "hockey stick" to drag the fallen one to safety. I hope to unravel the twisted ends of the lies that have sunken their roots into our mindset, and, perhaps free the reader from what I believe to be a curse on our land!

Section #1

The First Lie: Blessing Means Having

Preface To Lie #1

Mom gathered the five of us children around the little kitchen table. There glancing around at one another we prepared for the "treatment." My mother had practices she put us children through for "our good." We still look a little uncomfortably towards one another whenever the conversation comes up about those castor oil "affairs," and they bring an uneasy smile to our faces.

Caster Oil, mom thought, was to both cleanse us and prevent anything else from settling in. I hated the ordeal. We each sat at our places with a tablespoon full of Caster Oil in one hand, and an orange slice to chase the terrible taste away in the other. My technique was to do it all quickly. Just grab the spoon, take the medicine, and immediately stick the sweet nectar of orange into my mouth. In a short time the terrible taste of Castor Oil left my palate, and, as far as mom was concerned, I was "cleansed" and ready to go.

I realize that the next few chapters you read will not sit well with you at first. That is because they intend to be cathartic in nature. They are intended to cause reflection on God's Word, which is both the "Castor Oil" we resist, and the sweet "nectar" we long for.

We need a spiritual cleansing in our nation, a healing of our hearts. I think Americans have infused the cultural philosophy of our times with their spirituality. Frankly, I've been troubled lately by the way many Christians are speaking of God's blessing. Their way of thinking tends to be exclusive, limiting the goodness of God in the lives of believers by what is measured in terms unfamiliar to the Bible.

We are embracing in our culture a much different idea of blessing than what the Bible intended. We are encouraged to think big, expect the best, and wait for even more by the "Prosperity Gospel" being preached. Have we been brutally duped by being exposed to longer and deeper plunges into our world's system of belief than we have to our God's? The four chapters that follow challenge the first lie that is ruining our lives, namely, that God's blessing is the accumulation of things.

Chapter 1

Growing Up Poor

Is it true that the measure of God's blessing is in what we have? Joel Osteen writes in his book about how his wife wanted to buy a fancy house. He thought that wouldn't be possible, but states: "But Victoria had more faith. She convinced me we could live in an elegant home… and several years later, it did come to pass."[1]

That never happened to me. I was born in a small New England town, just about the time of the baby boom after WWII. My father had no money, and, like many men around that time, had to sell all he had to make it through the depression.

Because of my birth, he had to quickly piece together a little house he had been working on for awhile. Running low on time before my arrival, and having no funds to put in plumbing or a heating system, he concentrated on the basics, and soon moved my mother and four siblings into the four-room "shack."

Somehow, we got trapped into living in that shack, and for nearly sixteen years I lived without the luxury of an inside toilet or hot water to take a bath. Once a week, mom filled a galvanized container with water and heated it on the kerosene stove. Then we children, starting with the three oldest girls and my older brother, would take turns using it. Because I was the youngest,

I got the last opportunity. By the time my four other siblings had used it, there was a greasy film that had formed around the edges, and dirt swirled in the water.

I knew at an early age that we were different. The neighborhood that had grown up around my father's house was made up of a successful representation of society. Doctors, lawyers, and businessmen, these were the folks who lived in a development a few hundred feet from my father's meager home. Their children were my classmates, but none were my companions. We were out of place there, and I confronted that fact every day that I left for school.

I daydreamed about living in a beautiful house someday, a house with inside plumbing and a shower. I thought of how it would be to have one of those speakers at the front door to answer the doorbell when it rang, just like I had seen in many of those surrounding neighborhood homes. But mostly, I just wanted a place where I could invite a friend without embarrassment.

I had been embarrassed often by the shack. Our outside toilet facilities lacked cleanliness. Flies and spiders were bountiful, and the stench was breathtaking. I could never bring myself to invite a friend over, for fear he would need to use it!

Our living quarters were riddled with rodent holes. On one occasion, an insurance salesman came to collect a payment. As he stood at the front door, I was watching a little mouse dancing in and out of his hole, balancing precariously on the doorframe just above the man's head. I was a pre-school child then, but I knew the importance of keeping what I saw to myself. The salesman left with handshakes and smiles, knowing nothing of the incident that was happening just above his head. It was an early lesson in covering up the embarrassment of being poor, and cloaking it with silence and a smile.

My father tried to correct the rodent problem, but they seemed to survive by their sheer numbers. There were not only mice, but we were being overrun with rats. I remember hearing the traps going off all night on one occasion, as my father would get up to drown the rat that was caught and re-set the trap to do it all over again. By morning he had caught and drowned a dozen or so.

I dreaded school. I hated to face the ordeal of what another day of emotional abuse would bring. Word had gotten out that I was the kid who lived in the run-down shack that the busses drove by every day, the little one with no plumbing, busted up siding, and an outhouse on the side. I was subjected to a certain kind of prejudice based on my living condition, and ended up standing alone at recess, watching in envy while the others played baseball together, never being chosen on a team. I always ate lunch apart from the others. I remember wandering through the cafeteria with tray in hand, trying to find an empty section of table where I would be permitted to sit, normally where folks either didn't recognize me as the filthy kid from the shack, or just didn't care. There, far enough away from disgusted looks, I would take a seat in solitude as the "ugly Dickling," as I was called in reference to the nickname Dick that I was then using.

It was never the missing of material things that I regretted about being poor. It was that enigmatic process that slowly eats away at one's dignity and self-esteem, leaving you emotionally raped, and truly desperate for compassion. It was that feeling of being different and not belonging that put me to sleep in tears many nights as I grew up. Prejudice doesn't take choice into account. Most facing prejudice would choose to be someone different. It was not by choice I was born into a poor family, it is not by choice people are born into gender, color, or looks.

My father was a centered man, and a hard worker. Short and with a slender build, he had the pugnacity of a bulldog. Once, they had to humanely destroy a stubborn cow that was difficult to milk, being known for kicking the person milking her. My father grew tired of her constant irritation, and was determined to break her habit by retaliating with a punch of his own, but instead of breaking her habit he ended up breaking her leg.

The point is my father truly had determination. It wasn't by his carelessness that the ugly arm of "poorness" shackled him. If somehow punching back against the invisible leg that was constantly kicking against his dreams could have freed him and his family to a better lifestyle, he would have done so with grit and determination. But, poverty is like a quicksand. It slides you under little by little, until you are hopelessly deprived of economic life and breath. I call it asphyxiation by capitalization, where the wealthy get wealthier, while the poor slowly are pulled under by the invisible force of scarcity.

The land where my father built his little home lies dormant to this day, never having been used for commercial or any other reason for the past thirty-seven years. When visiting home, I go out of my way to go by that little spot, still resting in the center of a housing development and across the street from a strip mall. I pass by slowly, recognizing the large oak tree marking the old driveway. I wonder if it still bears the scars of when my mother ran into it when trying to learn to drive. Memories flood back to the "shack," but they are not pleasant, and I find myself glad once again to just leave it all behind as I speed away.

My father died relatively young, having lived out a difficult life. He was tired and in poor health. At the age of 54 he left us, leaving behind a wife and eight children, the youngest of who was just beginning school. I grieve for my three younger siblings, for though they never encountered the handicaps that those of us in the shack had, they never really were able to embrace experientially the lovely heritage my father had left behind. He was a man of honor and integrity.

My father found a source of spiritual strength and healing that was reflected in his life. I was proud of my father, not for what he achieved in life, but for what he achieved in spite of life. As Bebo Norman says:

> I will lift my eyes to the Maker
> Of the mountains I can't climb
> I will lift my eyes to the Calmer
> Of the oceans raging wild
> I will lift my eyes to the Healer
> Of the hurt I hold inside
> I will lift my eyes, lift my eyes to You[2]

My father had a hope for his family. Looking past the veil of poverty he saw a future for us, rich beyond measure, yet unseen by human eyes, and ultimately not of this world. He knew his children needed a Savior, not to rescue us from the diabolic grasp of poverty, but to rescue us from the lie that so often accompanies it.

That lie is structured around the belief that the blessing of God is equated with the good life, the land of milk and honey, so to speak. But I have had the privilege of understanding that lie and seeing its falsity revealed firsthand. I watched my father live poverty stricken as a blessed man. His life was not centered on "things," nor the craving after those. Instead, he gave to his wife and children his life, a moral compass to follow in the dark woods of ethical dilemmas.

Beyond the rides to the park and baseball games, he modeled integrity, and, he gave us the Light of hope for our future. He made some choices in life that have affected me, and the generations to follow after me. He directed my path in life through example and pattern. He brought me up in church. He lived morally clean. He taught me honesty, hard work, and the willingness to swear to my hurt.

A man cannot pass on his own spirituality to his children, but he can pass along the values that his spirituality has led him into. It's those values that create opportunity for God to work in. It's what I call a legacy of faith. It is that legacy of morality, a hope to be found outside of this world, and the need for God in my life which was passed along to me by my father. That legacy has been passed to my own children, whom I trust will pass the spiritual "torch" to their own. Someday, I foresee that lineage making up part of the New Jerusalem, that place where true values will surface; that place where no racial, economic, or social barriers exist. That same "hope" that my father had for his family, I've discovered is the hope that I have for mine. It is a hope they will find that success is not in the "things" we die taking, but in the things we die giving.

When I think back on those painful days of my youth, living among rodents the size of small cats, when dinner was a meal of corn mush three or four times a week, and when I would awaken in the morning without the privilege of being able to take a hot shower or bath, the words of Jesus come flooding back into my spirit, reminding me of a certain truth. It is those words that I want to end this chapter with, for they are words of both comfort and warning. They have formulated the principles that my father wrote upon my heart by example. Jesus said:

"'Blessed are you who are poor, for yours is the kingdom of God. Blessed are you who hunger now, for you will be satisfied. Blessed are you who weep now, for you will laugh. Blessed are you when men hate you, when they exclude you and insult you and reject your name as evil, because of the Son of Man. Rejoice in that day and leap for joy, because great is your reward in heaven. For that is how their fathers treated the prophets. But woe to you who are rich, for you have already received your comfort. Woe to you who are well fed now, for you will go hungry. Woe to you who laugh now, for you will mourn and weep.'" (Luke 6:20 25 NIV).

I am moved by both the dread of that Word and simultaneously, by its comfort. May those of us Christians who are driven to have what the world has take heed. And may those Christians who at this hour ponder that they may have missed the blessing of God be comforted in realizing that the blessing of God is not linked to the material, but to the spiritual.

"Blessing Means Having"

Small Group Discussion Questions
Chapter One Review

1. Have you ever been told, possibly in church, that a blessed person is one that has material wealth?

2. Name something better to leave behind as your legacy than an example of honesty, a strong work ethic, and faith.

3. Do you think it's easier to be poor when all around you are poor?

4. Have you ever felt different because of what you either did or did not have?

5. Where do you see yourself or your family in ten years? Spiritually? Financially?

6. Has your focus ever been on the "American Dream" more than the Kingdom of God?

Being Satisfied in a Land of Plenty

There was an old beer commercial that reminded its listeners to "reach for the gusto," that is, "the good life." In our culture, the good life is pictured as a life of plenty, filled with "things" and pleasure. As the bumper sticker says: "He who dies with the most toys wins." Is that what it takes to be satisfied with life? My father's example taught me that satisfaction does not come from reaching for the gusto.

There's been a lot of talk recently about corporate restructure. Microsoft has been in the news for years now. Enron made its fatal mistakes, leaving the Arthur Anderson accounting firm reeling in its wake. Shortly after, WorldCom made it to the front pages of the business section of newspapers everywhere with their own scandal. These things hit with such economic force, that Congress set up a task force known as the Public Company Accounting Oversight Board to ensure the safety of our financial structure. In a state of the union address, the president said they were "holding corporate criminals to account."[3] We are witnessing the downside of free enterprise; the inexplicable way in which sinful hearts will do all they can to gain all they want, regardless of who they hurt. Even Pope John said in a sermon before he died that the number one problem facing the world, and specifically the United States, is "unabated capitalism." And, the secretary of the National Council of Churches, Rev. Robert W. Edgar, said: "Jesus was not a capitalist; check out what [He] says about how hard it is to get to heaven if you're a rich man."[4]

We are capitalists, living in a land of plenty, and, as good as that gets, there are some interesting negative side effects to our industry. Capitalism in itself is not the problem, any more than money in itself is the problem. It is the love of money that is the problem, and it is the love of capitalism that is the problem as well.

The love of capitalism has sparked despair in the hearts of those that have tried, but failed, to have the good life. Everyone wants to go for the gusto, a piece of the good life. We look around to see what others have, and often come away thinking most everyone else has more. Parity is almost never realized, and therefore either crime or extra hard work becomes the equalizer. Borrowers became enslaved to their lenders, and loans are defaulted on. Living for a long time in that mental environment produces discouragement, frustration, and pessimism.

Don't believe in the lie. The lie says that the "blessing of God" has to do with economics. The fact is, many Christians who would not normally make that statement really do embrace that concept. They mix the idea of having more, with blessing. When we get a "windfall," we thank God for His favor, and for being so good to us. There seems to be a fine line here, for if God's blessing and favor are defined by the "things" we have, then Christians outside of the sphere of "having," such as those living in third world countries, would have to be considered less blessed and less in favor with God.

Compare that with what the Bible says. In speaking to the

church of Laodicea the angel says: "You say, 'I am rich; I have acquired wealth and do not need a thing.' But you do not real-ize that you are wretched, pitiful, poor, blind and naked." (Rev 3:17 NIV). In contrast, He says to the church of Smyrna: "I know your afflictions and your poverty yet you are rich!" (Rev 2:9 NIV). It's an interesting twist to most of our thinking. Having in the physical realm, does not equal having in the spiritual realm.

The idea is that we need to interpret God's blessing more accurately and appropriately. While blessing somehow inter-weaves with provision and preservation, it does not necessarily mean abundance. For example, there was just enough manna to last the Israelites from day to day. The people were not permit-ted to store it for future use. Trusting in God, the people were blessed, and had enough to eat. God was the perpetual source of provision and preservation.

I went to work that dreadful morning like I had done dozens of times before. I was driving a school bus because the job fit nicely into my college schedule. When I arrived, the boss greeted me, and introduced me to an individual she had with her. "He'll be riding with us today," she said. And off we went to pick up students for school.

In the process of that morning school bus run, as I eaves-dropped on the conversation between my boss and the individ-ual she had with her, I suddenly realized that this person I met was about to replace me at my job. The thought of that prospect sickened me. I was already behind on rent, and had little money to properly care for my wife and son. We drove back to the bus parking lot and she turned to the individual who had been rid-ing with us saying: "Show up in the morning, and you can drive this route."

Her words kicked in an adrenaline flow of panic. I desperately needed the job. A friend gave me a ride home that morning, and I told him what had happened, but it didn't seem like a major concern to him. It felt major to me. Nothing going on around me seemed to be as important as me losing my job! I felt like someone had kicked me in the stomach. My mind was whirling, as I staggered through the door, dragged myself into the nearby bedroom, and collapsed to my knees at the foot of my little son's bed. Though he wasn't home, somehow I wanted to be near him, realizing that I was letting him down, leaving him devoid of the substances that make up a good father, depriving him of the things any man needs to give his children.

I wept bitterly before God that morning. I felt desperate and alone. The demands on my life as a young husband and father seemed overwhelming. How would I tell my wife the bad news? How long would it take to pack everything up and leave school?

My throat ached with the pain of crying as I plead for God to "heal" my situation. Somehow through the madness of my racing mind, God whispered a gentle thought to me that morning. "Open the Bible," he said into my spirit.

From my knees I grabbed the nearest Bible to me and began to read from the pages that had inexplicably fallen open as I laid it before me:

"Therefore I tell you, do not worry about your life, what you will eat or drink; or about your body, what you will wear. Is not life more important than food, and the body more important than clothes? Look at the birds of the air; they do not sow or reap or store away in barns, and yet your heavenly Father feeds them. Are you not much more valuable than they? Who of you by worrying can add a single hour to his life? And why do you worry about clothes? See how the lilies of the field grow. They do not labor or spin. Yet I tell you that not even Solomon in all his splendor was dressed like one of these. If that is how God clothes the grass of the field, which is here today and tomorrow is thrown into the fire, will he not much more clothe you, O you of little faith? So do not worry, saying, 'What shall we eat?' or 'What shall we drink?' or 'What shall we wear?' For the pagans run after all these things, and your heavenly Father knows that you need them. But seek first his kingdom and his righteousness, and all these things will be given to you as well." (Mat 6:25-33 NIV).

We are His sheep, what an interesting truth! I promised God that morning that I would stay within His consignment for my life, and that I would trust Him to create a way. My boss offered the job to the person she had with her that day. He only needed to show up the next morning, but, he never did! That same young man ran into my wife about two years later where she worked. In blank conversation, she mentioned that I was attending a nearby college, studying to become a pastor, and driving a school bus to support us. With incredulity his eyes widened as he described what I looked like to my wife. "I almost took his job," he related to her, "but something wouldn't let me do it." My wife knew that the something was really a Someone!

The blessing of God comes when we are obedient to stay within the parameters of God's "place" for our lives. Those parameters undoubtedly change from time to time as God adjusts them, but, the blessed people of God throughout the Bible were men and women who stayed within those strictures set by God.

The unfortunate thing for Christians living in the "land of

plenty" is that we tend to create our own "blessing," and attribute it to God. Our "blessing" then becomes the result of what we crave. That mistake hinges on a determination of God that we often overlook. God has allowed us the freedom of choice! He has not created us to be automatons. Consequently, our own desires often supersede God's desire for our lives. In other words, it is God's will to permit that our choices will sow into what our lives will reap.

A good example of God's permissive will is found within the political structure of ancient Israel. There was a time in the nation's life that they begged for a king, and so they said to the prophet Samuel: "…You are old, and your sons do not walk in your ways; now appoint a king to lead us, such as all the other nations have." (I Sam 8:5 NIV). The fact is, God's ultimate will was that He would be their King and that the nation be recognized as a Theocracy. But in His permissive will, He allowed their choices to determine their future. Therefore, the Scripture in I Samuel continues: "But when they said, "Give us a king to lead us," this displeased Samuel; so he prayed to the LORD. And the LORD told him: "Listen to all that the people are saying to you; it is not you they have rejected, but they have rejected me as their king." (I Sam 8:6 7 NIV). God's decreed will ultimately supersedes all others, but, within the confines of this life, God allows mankind the freedom of choice.

Jim Bakker, former minister and television host of the PTL Club who resigned after revelations of accounting fraud, was eventually imprisoned. But what was the real reason for his public defrocking? Peel away the legal ruling, and you're primarily left with this: Jim Bakker believed that the blessing of God was increasing his empire. In reality it was his lack of contentment that was increasing it. I'm certain that this man of God has learned a costly lesson, indicative by his book "I Was Wrong." A lesson that many of us have yet to learn, for many of us bear similar interests in our own hearts, as we confuse the blessing of God with having.

The apostle Paul brings us this reminder from his own experience: "...I have learned to be content whatever the circumstances. I know what it is to be in need, and I know what it is to have plenty. I have learned the secret of being content in any and every situation, whether well fed or hungry, whether living in plenty or in want. I can do everything through him who gives me strength." (Phil 4:11–13 NIV).

My understanding is that the blessing of God comes from staying within the parameters He has established for our lives. It is controlled under His will for us, by His loving choice, and in that we can remain content. Slipping beneath the surging "waves" of want that so often roll over us only leads to drowning in negativism and defeat.

From time to time it is good to remind ourselves that this place we live is not our home. We are citizens of a place that the Bible calls "heaven." [cf. Phil 3.20]. This Greek word for heaven is *ouranos,* derived from the Greek *oros,* meaning to rise above, and refers to a place beyond the earth. *Ouranos* is figuratively, and, by implication, the abode of God.[5]

This is not the place of our final destiny. It is not the same "Kingdom of God" to be established at Christ's return. This place called heaven is rather a spiritual habitation beyond the confines of this earth. It is a place one arrives at through a relationship with Christ, it cannot be located on a map, nor can we be physically transported to it. It is *ouranos,* a place where we meet Christ spirit to Spirit. It is more genuine than what we touch, taste, or see, for the physical components of our bodies cannot deceive us there. It is real, and it is truth because God is there, and from that place directs His people. As Jesus taught: "This, then, is how you should pray: "'Our Father in heaven, hallowed be your name, your kingdom come, your will be done on earth as it is in heaven. (Mat 6:9–10 NIV)

It is as citizens of this "*ouranos*" that we eagerly wait for Christ's return to earth. Our hearts, thoughts, and actions should therefore be motivated to remember what our citizenship is all about, and, it is not about gathering those "blessings" which are limited to, and anchor us, to this earth.

The question probably should be posed: Do you believe this? Apparently the apostle Paul did, for he says: "…I consider everything a loss compared to the surpassing greatness of knowing Christ Jesus my Lord, for whose sake I have lost all things. I consider them rubbish, that I may gain Christ" (Phil 3:8 NIV).

The problem is in transferring what we believe into what we live. I theorize that Christians need to be "wrecked" before that transference comes, before they can discover that they don't belong to the spiritual, political, and economic patterns of this world.

The Apostle Paul had been "wrecked." Having been there at the stoning of Stephen, he watched over the coats that were placed in his care, and heard Stephen pray to the One he had been persecuting: "… 'Lord Jesus, receive my spirit.' Then he fell on his knees and cried out, 'Lord, do not hold this sin against them…'" (Acts 7:59-60 NIV).

Confused and tormented over the prospect that this Jesus whom Stephen prayed to, and that he was persecuting, might be the Messiah Lord of the Old Testament, he traveled on to

Damascus. It was on that road that he saw a light from heaven "brighter than the sun," and heard a voice calling to him from its midst. [cf. Acts 26.13–14].

It was an experience that left him blind and submissive to God. He had been "wrecked," and in that state called out meekly to the voice he was hearing: "Who are you, Lord?" The voice from the light replied: "I am Jesus, whom you are persecuting" [cf. Acts 26.15].

Paul was "wrecked" because in his conscience he was fighting. He saw the good man Stephen pleading to God for the forgiveness of those stoning him. His spiritual "sonar" was pinging back to him a confirmation of truth concerning what Stephen and others had been saying about Jesus. That is why the great Heart Knower calling to Paul from the light said, "…It is hard for you to kick against the goads." [Note: A goad is a cactus-like plant] (Acts 26:14 NIV).

From that moment on, Paul's citizenship was in heaven and not earth. Reading about his sacrificial journey for the sake of ministry to others is humbling. He was beaten, stoned, misunderstood by both the Jews and Gentiles; he was stripped of dignity, and left for dead by those he hoped would understand his message. All of his passion turned toward "the greatness of knowing" his Messiah Lord. Things of this life paled in comparison to that. It turns out, Paul considered himself a blessed man at the end of his life, in spite of all he gave up: "I have fought the good fight, I have finished the race, I have kept the faith. Now there is in store for me the crown of righteousness …" (2 Tim 4:7-8 NIV).

Fact is, most of the Biblical personalities that had a passion after God had gone through a time of being "wrecked."

That is, they came to a point in their lives when they realized their desire to be part of the *ouranos,* as a citizen of heaven, was greater than their desire to be part of the political, economical, and spiritual pattern of this world.

The love for money, or even capitalism, seems to be the opposite view of that. Reaching for all the gusto you can, while you can, is in apparent disharmony with the Biblical view. It is misunderstanding the sense of God's blessing. In so doing, we become focused on what our hearts yearn after. Being focused on the things offered in this world system only lead to disappointment in the end. If you want to stay positive in a downward spiraling materialistic environment, you must come to a point of realization that this "land of plenty" is not where you belong, but that your citizenship is in heaven. It's all about choices, and, what you choose will determine your focus, and, what you focus on will determine your contentment.

That point is well illustrated by the man who wanted to get rich quickly. He walked into a jewelry store in one of the local malls. It was in the middle of the day, crowds of people were shopping all around, and mall security was everywhere. He walked over to the nearest counter, where gold watches were exhibited under a locked glass display. Without hesitation he reached under his trench coat and pulled out a brick. Slamming the brick through the glass display, he proceeded to gather up all the gold watches, and place them into a satchel he was carrying.

Alarms went off everywhere, the store manager called security, and within mere seconds, he was handcuffed and carted off by mall security. He was placed in a police car, and rushed to the local police headquarters, where a detective placed him under arrest and asked him a few questions.

"I don't understand", the detective queried. "Why would you attempt to rob a jewelry store in the middle of the day, in a crowded mall, where security is all around? Weren't you afraid of getting caught?" The beleaguered frustrated thief simply replied, "I didn't see whether it was day or night, I didn't see the crowd of people shopping nearby, nor did I see any mall security, I just saw the gold!"

My father was never blinded by focusing on the "gold" of life. That focus is a lie, and can lead to desperate acts, discouragement, or the feeling of spiritual deprivation. It's hard to see God's blessing through an assiduous economical philosophy of life. In fact, I dare say, if you're aggressively lusting after fortune, I think in the end, to be made complete, you will have to sell it all, to follow Jesus.

A life of full surrender in the spiritual realm cannot have ties to the things of this life. Remember the man who approached Jesus as He was leaving the region of Judea? He ran to Jesus, falling to his knees before Him in great humility and sincerity saying, "What must I do to inherit eternal life?" Jesus in response pointed to the moral laws that governed man's relationship to man, such as, honesty, integrity, adultery, stealing, and honoring one's parents.

This man had a soft heart towards God, and with full sincerity assured Jesus that he had kept those commands since he was a child. Furthermore, God's heart was soft towards him, for the Bible notes that:

"Jesus looked at him and loved him. 'One thing you lack,' he said. 'Go, sell everything you have and give to the poor, and you will have treasure in heaven. Then come, follow me.' At this the man's face fell. He went away sad, because he had great wealth. Jesus looked around and said to his disciples, 'How hard it is for the rich to enter the kingdom of God!'" (Mark 10:21–23 NIV).

Sadly, note the words that are not included in that text. Jesus didn't rush after him. He didn't assure him that in time things would work themselves out. He didn't beg him to come back, to reconsider, or to take one small step at a time. He simply let him go! God allows you to choose!

I've heard it said: "It's okay to have "things," just don't let them have you." The scary thing is that we usually can't tell when the "things" in our lives have taken over. For example, most everyone would say that an occasional cookie is absolutely okay. But for me, once turns to more frequent times, and frequency turns to lust! To stay healthy, my wife and I refuse to have certain foods in the house. It's easier to stay focused on our health when the temptation to eat something unhealthy is removed.

I really believe that same principle holds true spiritually. It's easier to stay focused on heavenly things when earthly temptations are removed. Here's my point, both Abraham and Lot were wealthy, both were apparently righteous before God, but something happened to Lot. Was it okay for Lot to have his "cookie?" Lot didn't know the "cookie" would turn to insatiable desire. How could he have? There was something in him that he couldn't turn loose until it made him "fat" to the world and "skinny" toward God.

Consider the story of Elijah. He had settled into the Kerith Ravine after telling the king there would be no rain for the next several years. God sent him hiding, promising to supply his needs from a brook he was to drink from and the ravens God would send to bring him food. But, after some time, the brook dried up and God sent Elijah packing towards Zarephath.

This is where the story gets interesting for me. Zarephath, from the Hebrew Zaraph, meaning to refine, was the place he met the widow. This widow is an interesting character in the Bible. If you're not careful you slip by an important spiritual truth that is modeled by this woman. Elijah strolls up to her, weary from the hundred mile journey in the desert. He's quite a character himself. Weather worn, his tanned skin glistening in the sun, hair flailing in the wind, stroking his unkempt beard, he beckoned to her through sun baked lips: " ..."Would you bring me a little water in a jar so I may have a drink?" {11} As she was going to get it, he called, "And bring me, please, a piece of bread." (1 Ki 17:10–11 NIV).

Now look at this widow. She was obviously familiar with pain, trying to raise a son without a husband. She was emptied of emotion, having grieved over death before; she now was out gathering sticks to make a fire for a final meal to feed her son. She was poor and pitiful! Amazingly, she was the supply that God would use to care for Elijah. Zarephath, the place of refining, must have been intended for both Elijah and the widow.

> "As surely as the Lord your God lives," she replied, "I don't have any bread—only a handful of flour in a jar and a little oil in a jug. I am gathering a few sticks to take home and make a meal for myself and my son, that we may eat it—and die." {13} Elijah said to her, "Don't be afraid. Go home and do as you have said. But first make a small cake of bread for me from what you have and bring it to me, and then make something for yourself and your son. {14} For this is what the Lord, the

God of Israel, says: 'The jar of flour will not be used up and the jug of oil will not run dry until the day the Lord gives rain on the land.'" (1 Ki 17:12–14 NIV).

Elijah asked the widow the same thing that Jesus asked the rich young man; "will you give God everything?" It must have stopped this widow cold! That request would result in her death! There you have it, that tidbit of truth summed up in the example of the widow, that God wants to exhaust all of our own resources, leading to our death, that we may have all of Him. As Paul said: "I have been crucified with Christ and I no longer live, but Christ lives in me ..." (Gal 2:20 NIV).

Whether one is the rich young man or the poor widow, the liberating focus is in allowing God to have it all. Perhaps more importantly, God will require of us an account of the resources he gives us stewardship over. This widow, the unlikely source for Elijah's supply, was tapped on the shoulder by God. He wanted access to her, or better, His resources. If she refused, if she craved to hold on to "things," or if her focus was on her "things," would she have run out of flour and oil? Her example to us is powerful; if you release to God what you have, your supply will never lack: "She went away and did as Elijah had told her. So there was food every day for Elijah and for the woman and her family. {16} For the jar of flour was not used up and the jug of oil did not run dry, in keeping with the word of the LORD spoken by Elijah. (1 Ki 17:15–16 NIV).

When you crave the things that this world offers, it indicates that the "something" in you that is unwilling to forgo the "cookie" will be difficult to control. That was what Jesus was preparing the wealthy young man for. Remember, he wanted to know how to get tighter with God. While you can be either rich or poor and have the wrong focus, "focus bending" is easier done to you when you keep the "cookie" in your house! Or, as Jesus said: "It is easier for a camel to go through the eye of a needle than for a rich man to enter the kingdom of God." (Mark 10:25 NIV).

Do a mental exercise. Between the apostle Paul and the rich young man, who do you envision making it into God's Kingdom, without question? How about this rich young man, did he eventually make it? He probably did, don't you think? But, there is more of a question over him than over Paul, because Paul never lost his focus!

The tendency is to say there are no easy answers to this. I would rather believe there are no easy questions. It's tough to ask ourselves about our spending. It's tough to ask ourselves about how we as Christians should live in this age of consumerism. When do we have enough "things?" Is the new car necessary? What would Jesus do?

It's hard for me to explain. Most of those people reading this can do a better job than I. But, I see a principle in Scripture, and as I compare that to our culture, most Christians in America don't have what the widow had. Instead, we are much more like the rich young man! Whether in times of need or plenty, you must trust God and hold loosely whatever you have in your hand!

It's hard to hold things loosely unless you're satisfied with what God has given you. We were going through financial hardship at college. We couldn't keep up with rent, baby supplies, and groceries. On one occasion, something had to give, and for that week we literally had nothing left to eat. We were hungry that chilly fall night in the Berkshires, when we sat down around the table. It was bare, along with the cabinets and fridge. Our funds were totally exhausted. I suggested we give thanks anyway for God's supply. Holding the hand of my hungry wife, we gently bowed our hearts before our Master. In pure honesty we acknowledged our hunger before God, yet, assured Him of our contentment to rest within his resources for us. "If You choose to not supply food," we asked, "then stave off the hunger that is ripping at our stomachs."

Barely had those words surfaced from our hearts, when a knock on the door disrupted our prayer. It was a buddy from next door. He had a question to ask, and we sat around for several minutes just chatting about nothing. Shortly, he got up to leave, opened the door, and turned back sharply on his way out. "You better bring these groceries in," he called, "they're starting to freeze out here." I want to make clear to you that we saw no one come with that box of groceries. They would have been easily spotted if they had. And, it wasn't there a short time earlier when we came home. I knew God had placed them there for our provision.

The box was loaded with canned meats, vegetables, and powdered potatoes. We were yearning for mashed potatoes, so my wife fixed them up, and served them on the plates. Pink potatoes! That's what they were! That was God's supply! Initially, I was unhappy with that supply, I had never had pink potatoes before. Had they gone rancid? And then it hit me, just a few minutes earlier we were sitting at an empty table when God heard our cries. This truly was His supply of pink potatoes, not only good, but truly most delicious indeed! I've had many "pink potatoes" since then, and all have proven to be excellent.

Satisfaction with God's best. That's really it, isn't it? The more satisfied you are with God's best, the more satisfied you are with "pink potatoes." Have you ever been "wrecked?" Have you ever been absolutely desperate for God? If not, you will most likely never stay satisfied with His place for you in this land of plenty. You must dispose of the lie concerning God's blessing. It is not about having the material things of this earth.

Two words in the New Testament Greek are translated as blessing. The first word, *"makarios"*, is found in the beatitudes: "Blessed are the poor in spirit... Blessed are those who mourn... Blessed are the meek... ," etc. [cf. Mat 5:3-5]. *Makarios* means well off or fortunate. By implication it is a state of being, as in: "...we must help the weak, remembering the words the Lord Jesus himself said: 'It is more blessed to give than to receive." (Acts 20:35 NIV)[6]

The second word, *eulogia* is found in the following samplings: "Land that drinks in the rain often falling on it and that produces a crop useful to those for whom it is farmed receives the blessing of God." (Heb 6:7 NIV). Or again: "When God made his promise to Abraham, since there was no one greater for him to swear by, he swore by himself, saying, 'I will surely bless you and give you many descendants.'" (Heb 6:13-14 NIV).[7]

The Greek *eulogia* is where the English word eulogy comes from. A eulogy is a speech or writing that praises another, associated with the good things said at funerals. *Eulogia* is combination of two other Greek words. *"Eu"* which means good or well, and *"logos"* which means something said, or something reasoned. When God blesses us, He says or reasons something good on our behalf. Our inheritance through Christ is God's speaking and acting well towards us. As Peter said: "...to this you were called so that you may inherit a blessing." (1 Pet 3:9 NIV).

Neither Greek word translated as blessing necessarily has to do with having in the material sense. It is much rather understood as being in a place where God looks favorably upon your life; that is, when He speaks, acts, and reasons well toward you. It is not in reaching for the gusto, it is not in having the material things of this world system, it is in simply knowing that we are under the gentle Hand of God, for our good. You will never stay satisfied until you dispose of the lie concerning God's blessing, and embrace your real citizenship.

"Blessing Means Having"

Small Group Discussion Questions
Chapter Two Review

1. How can someone or a group of people have afflictions and poverty, yet be rich? (See Revelations 2:9)

2. Has your attention ever been on wealth or the "American Dream," rather than on the Kingdom of God?

3. How has God provided for you during the famines of life? Were you able to find peace in God's provision?

4. Have you ever contemplated your citizenship in heaven? What are the privileges of citizenship?

5. In what ways is it harder for a rich man to enter the Kingdom of God?

6. How would you contrast the blessing of a Christian in our country with that of a believer in a third world country?

Dissatisfaction Leads
To Discouragement

The product of dissatisfaction is discouragement. It actually happens quite easily in the atmosphere of an aggressive economic mindset. Folks have come to believe what they have heard on television, or read in magazines, concerning the pictures and promises of success and opportunity. Newlyweds no longer have a need to save money for years before buying that first home, as was the case just a generation ago. Not so much is required from the borrower these days, not so much down payment or personal investment. Things have changed maybe even for the better, but, there's always a price for change, and, in this case, the price for easy borrowing can lead to dissatisfaction and opens the door to discouragement.

I like the commercial on television that shows a middle-aged man riding in his vehicle, describing all the things he owns. In the background you see a beautiful home. He pulls up into the driveway to an immaculately cared for yard with beautiful flowers and shrubs. Then, stepping out of the car, he describes his membership at the plush country club. After telling of his gains and accomplishments he says smiling cheerfully: "And how did I do it? I'm in debt up to my eyeballs! Please, somebody help me."

Many Americans can relate to his dilemma, over their heads owing to the "system" of wanting and getting. The following statistics point that out:

The average American household has 13 payment cards

There are 1.3 billion payment cards in circulation in the United States.

Americans carry, on average, $5,800 in credit card debt from month to month.

Over 40% of US families spend more than they earn.

Almost one out of every 100 households in the US will file for bankruptcy.

92% of U.S. family disposable income is spent on paying debts.[8]

The lie has led many to believe that the accumulation of things can somehow make an individual happier, but, there just are never enough things in the world to satisfy a persons craving to please the self. Add to one's craving the media perception that everyone else has, does, or enjoys more than us, and, you have the recipe for discouragement. Discouragement comes along if you hope to be equal to the perceived world around you, and somehow find yourself either unable to do so, or drowning in debt because you tried.

The truth is that we all have discouraging "tunnels" that we drive through, but our world view will determine how we come out on the other end. It is God's world view that gives us the only hope of contentment when no light seems to be shining through.

Strangely, it was discouragement that forced a man named Gideon to rediscover God's provision in his life. His story centers on a hopeless situation. It was roughly one thousand years before Christ was born. The nation of Israel had entered into the Promised Land, but generally was not following after God. There was no real leadership to turn to; no King was in place over the people. These people, God's people, Gideon's family, were incurring a terrible onslaught by a ravaging enemy. Desperate for protection, they chose to live in the caves and dens of the hills surrounding their little town.

The enemy, in the form of a few surrounding nations, was attacking their source of livelihood. In numbers too many to count, they marched against the land, trampling down the ripened harvest in their path, taking the best of their livestock, and leaving God's people starved and despondent. Listen to the following description: "Whenever the Israelites planted their crops, the Midianites, Amalekites and other eastern peoples invaded the country. They camped on the land and ruined the crops all the way to Gaza and did not spare a living thing for Israel, neither sheep nor cattle nor donkeys. They came up with their livestock and their tents like swarms of locusts. It was impossible to count the men and their camels; they invaded the land to ravage it." (Judg 6:3-5 NIV).

Change the time period and name of the enemy, and it could echo the story of many American Christians today. They are being ravaged at the root of their economics. They live from paycheck to paycheck, and hope that nothing disrupts the pattern of earning and spending. If a car breaks down or a new appliance is needed, it is disastrous to their financial picture. To magnify the problem, they perceive their situation as never getting better, even though the blessing "lie" tells them otherwise. They feel they are being chased from their own homes, desperately in need of help and protection.

Having said that, there is yet hope; God speaks to us in the midst of disconsolate darkness. The story of Gideon shows us five things about discouragement, and a conclusion that rivets us to the heart of God, and God alone.

#1 Discouragement is the product of spiritual distraction

"Midian so impoverished the Israelites that they cried out to the Lord for help. When the Israelites cried to the Lord because of Midian, he sent them a prophet, who said, "This is what the Lord, the God of Israel, says: I brought you up out of Egypt, out of the land of slavery. I snatched you from the power of Egypt and from the hand of all your oppressors. I drove them from before you and gave you their land. I said to you, 'I am the Lord your God; do not worship the gods of the Amorites, in whose land you live.' But you have not listened to me." (Ju 6: 6–10 NIV).

The question is begging to be asked; why had all this happened to the people of God? The answer is revealing. God's people got caught up and distracted by the lifestyle and "gods" of the land in which they were living. They had forgotten about the God who rescued them from slavery to Egypt, the God who powerfully freed them from the hands of their oppressors, and who miraculously brought them to the land in which they were now living.

Because a man cannot serve two masters, they made their allegiance with the "gods" of the land where they lived. But, the "gods" of the land were not the true Creator, and proved unfaithful and deceitful to them. Unfortunately, because they believed the lie, they lost the protection and provision of the true and living God. Consequently, their "things" were getting eaten up and taken over by the enemy.

I know that to be true with many of my Christian friends. They have listened to the lies of the land they live in, and have been robbed of a joyful, peaceful economy. Steeped in the mindset of the land, their sole aim is to attain and hold on to the "things" which seem most relevant to them. It is no wonder that because they have played into the hands of the enemy, he is eating up their wealth, joy, and peace. God stirs us to keep Him first in our lives.

As Israel became desperate due to her evaporating resources, when the throes of starvation had finally settled in, she cried in resignation to the true God. In His mercy, God spoke to them clearly and undeniably through the voice of a prophet. The indication is that God wanted them to know the reason for their suffering: "you have not listened to Me."

When the Christian wanders away from God's best, the God of mercy will stop them in their tracks by speaking with an undeniably clear voice. It is as though He offers a last chance effort to regain our attention and respect. I think of an example of that when I was quite young.

My mother had told me never to cross the street on my own. We lived next to a fairly busy road, the main thoroughfare between two little towns. When I started first grade at school, my bus stop was also where the town parked their busses at the end of the day. It was just a few hundred feet from where we lived, and mom, knowing my venturesome spirit gave explicit instructions for me not to deviate from my destination to or from that bus stop.

One afternoon, after returning home from school, I realized I had forgotten something very "important" on the bus. I hung around in the adjacent neighbor's driveway waiting for the bus to return after the driver finished his last stop. I watched as the bus made the final turn into the parking spot, and the driver stepped out. I was focused, and the temptation was strong.

My mind wrestled with a decision to either disobey my mother or to just go home. I reasoned that since my mother's admonition I had gotten much older, and anyhow, it was only a short distance away. I knew I could get across and back before my mother ever found out, but, I also knew it would be wrong!

As the lure of the bus grew stronger, I began to take the first step to cross the road. It was then that I heard my name being called out in an emphatically clear and undeniable manner. It absolutely stopped me cold in my tracks. I wheeled around to face whomever it was that had caught my disobedience, but there was no one there!

I was relieved to have not gotten caught, but realized even in my child's heart that God had heard my inner struggle with sin, and was giving me a last chance opportunity to repent. And repent I did, as I turned away from the edge of the road and walked away, like a dog with his tail between his legs.

It was that unmistakably "loud and clear" voice sent from God that stopped me from continuing in my sin; like the voice of a prophet to His people. As I ponder that memory as an adult, I wonder what danger may have occurred if I chose to disobey God's unquestionable warning. I have never heard God's audible voice again, but He still confronts my spiritual distraction with a word that stops me in my tracks. It might be by way of a sermon, a "nudging" of my heart during a time of worship, or by seeing a reflection of my character in a Bible verse, that He reminds me to remain focused on obedience to Him.

Discouragement is the product of spiritual distraction. God confronts that distraction by stopping us in our tracks, reminding us of His Word through the "prophet," but we must be willing to obey what our heart has heard. That truth underlines every decision we make, whether moral, spiritual, or financial. We must not become distracted by the lure of the land, and thus keep our spiritual ears sensitive to God.

2 Discouragement is a pivotal point for spiritual failure or success

"The angel of the Lord came and sat down under the oak in Ophrah that belonged to Joash the Abiezrite, where his son Gideon was threshing wheat in a winepress to keep it from the Midianites. When the angel of the Lord appeared to Gideon, he said, 'The Lord is with you, mighty warrior.'" (Ju 6: 11–12 NIV).

Gideon is not a picture of faith and spirituality as we read of him threshing out wheat in the privacy and cover of a winepress, hiding from the Midianites. Yet, God calls him "mighty warrior." At first glance, you might even accuse God of sarcasm, but look a little further for the truth. God wasn't referring to the man we see cowering, but rather the spiritual man of potential that lay somewhere under the surface in Gideon. The man God saw really was a mighty warrior, just a bit battle weary and worn from the wounds of discouragement.

The angel's confidence in Gideon seems to be a wake up call. God is letting this bruised warrior know that it's time he grab hold of himself and get on with the purpose at hand. It seems to me that there's a time God says to the defeated Christian, "come on, get hold of yourself, it's time to get on with the walk."

I have a friend living in Vermont who is a computer technician. While I was the pastor of a church there, I would call on him with my computer woes. On one occasion, I had pulled up a series of odd files. Because they didn't appear to be doing anything, or make much sense to me as I read their titles, I figured I'd push the button reading "Yes" when the machine asked if I wanted to delete them.

I was soon on the phone calling my friend for help. He told me I had wiped out some necessary files, hidden in the "brains," that the computer needed to "boot up." Being an unfamiliar term to me at the time, I asked what it meant to "boot up" a computer. His explanation has stayed with me through the years, for it has a spiritual application as well.

Drawing a diagram of a tree trunk with branches, he explained that a computer reaches down its "trunk" file by file, searching for the various branches, or files, that the computer is programmed to look for when turned on. The process, he said, is much like pulling a boot up from the bottom of your leg, hence the term "booting up." These significant files were the ones I had inadvertently wiped out; they were the ones the computer needed to "come to life."

"Grabbing yourself by the bootstraps" is a term we use to suggest that we need to get on with it, to come to life so to speak. Spiritually speaking, there is a time for us to reach down to find all that we have been "programmed" by God to operate by. That supernatural "programming" brings us to spiritual "life," reminding us to view things from God's perspective.

The angel of the Lord spoke a challenge to Gideon: "God is with you, mighty warrior." The implication is immense. God was throwing Gideon's switch on, and, in computer terminology, it was time for him to either "crash" or "boot up." If it were true that God was with him, he had no need to keep hiding in the winepress.

It reminds me of the battle between Jesus and the devil in the wilderness. John had just baptized Jesus in the Jordan River when a voice from heaven said: "…'You are my Son, whom I love; with you I am well pleased.'" (Mark 1:11 NIV). The very next verse tells us that Jesus went immediately from that experience into the wilderness to be tempted by the devil for forty days. There, Jesus was tested as to what He would believe concerning what he was told by the audible voice of the Father.

The devil taunted Jesus over and over with this challenge: "If you are the Son of God." (cf. Mt 4.1-11). Jesus had come to a place where He needed to choose whether or not to believe it was the voice of the Father He had heard at the river. I think that experience in the wilderness was a pivotal point in His ministry. As with Gideon, it was a time that He needed to accept or reject the Father's assessment of Him.

In the end, Jesus was able to defeat the devil by reaching down to His "bootstraps," reminding the devil of what God said in Scripture, and believing the purpose for what He was called to do as the Messiah. All of us have a purpose from God that is at times challenged by the questioning lies of the devil. The point is, what will you believe? The answer to that is in knowing what God has "programmed" you with. Consider these words: "Now this is what the LORD Almighty says: 'Give careful thought to your ways. You have planted much, but have harvested little. You eat, but never have enough. You drink, but never have your fill. You put on clothes, but are not warm. You earn wages, only to put them in a purse with holes in it.'" (Hag 1:5–6 NIV).

This is what that means. When we give ourselves over to the purpose and focus of this world, we place our trust in something other than God. In doing so, we limit, or even prevent, God's best provision for our lives. Instead, we find ourselves at the mercy of this world system, and, when that happens, there will never be enough gold to satisfy, and our pockets will always be robbed by the enemy.

That had to be running through Gideon's mind. The nation had turned their back on God to follow the ways of the land they were living in. And now, here he was, trying to protect his sustenance from the enemy. Whimpering in a winepress, he was fearful, discouraged, and pretty much beaten by the enemy.

Maybe you have a worn out Gideon in you, battered by the enemy, discouraged by the financial mockery the devil has put you through. It's a pivotal point for you really. In the end, you will choose to listen to one of two things. You will heed either the twisted truth of the world saying: "you deserve, you need, you should have," so therefore, you will then take more, do more, and want more." Or perhaps you will recognize the voice of God deep within who has "programmed" you for a higher purpose. Perhaps you will look beyond your "outer" self, beyond the lusting for what this world offers, beyond the bruising caused by the financial whipping you've been taking. Perhaps you will look within, as God does, and see that in His eyes you really are a "mighty warrior!" Then you will hear the angel of the Lord whisper gently in your ear: "the Lord is with you." You don't have to stay hiding from the enemy in the winepress.

Gideon needed to reach down to his bootstraps, to "boot up" and believe God's word concerning him, the wounded warrior, and to accept those things that his inner computer had been programmed to look for. Discouragement comes when we choose to find "files" programmed there by the world, and not those programmed by God, it really is a pivotal point for us, one that will inscribe either our failure or success in the surroundings that we live.

#3 Discouragement leads to an unhealthy
questioning of God's faithfulness and love

"But sir," Gideon replied, "if the Lord is with us, why has all this happened to us? Where are all his wonders that our fathers told us about when they said, 'Did not the Lord bring us up out of Egypt?' But now the Lord has abandoned us and put us into the hand of Midian." (Ju 6.13).

Gideon must have been musing about Israel's past history, the testimonies that had been passed down through the generations. It was a mighty God who intervened when the nation was held under the bondage of Egypt. It was a powerful God behind little Moses when he confronted the Egyptian magicians. It was God the Creator who parted the forceful Red Sea so the Israelites could pass through to the other side. And, it was God Almighty who then closed that sea again upon the chariots and horsemen of the Egyptian army. God the Protector was seen by the people as He led them by a cloud during the day and a pillar of fire at night, while God the Provider fed them personally every morning with a strange, never before seen, item called Manna.

That's the kind of God Gideon knew in his heart, but, it was not what he currently was experiencing. Gideon's complaint to the angel was: "If the LORD is with us, why has all this happened to us?" It's a question that has been addressed to God throughout the centuries, "God, if you really loved me, why?" The words following "why" vary from person to person and from situation to situation. Sadly, we apply our understanding, or definition, of what is love and right to our situation, and then expect God to fit into that understanding. Consequently, when life isn't explained by our definition of right, or our understanding of love, we challenge God.

I'd say that was where Gideon was at: "why has all this happened to us?" I too challenged God for many years as a young man, "Why was I born into a poor family?" Or, "Why are there poor families at all?" Many who have lost loved ones well before their time, or through accidental death ask, "Why do bad things happen to good people?" Or, "Why do the innocent die?"

There's an answer to those questions that is a difficult spiritual truth. We live under the general umbrella of the reign of Satan, the "prince of this world." (cf. Jn 12.31). He is the author of death and the cause of despair: "When Adam sinned, sin entered the entire human race. Adam's sin brought death, so death spread to everyone, for everyone sinned." (Rom 5:12 NLT).

Here's the point. God made us "in His image," that is, with having similar attributes to Himself, including, the ability to choose. The "doorway" to Satan was opened by the choices of Adam, who chose to listen to Satan over God. But also remember, "Everyone sinned." It is in our nature to do what Adam did. We would have made the same choices that Adam made!

Yet, God has not abandoned us to our sin. That is the Good News message. He gave us a surprising way to discover our failures. He exposed our need of help through His ten commands. Who could live by them? The apostle Paul said: "God's law was given so that all people could see how sinful they were. But as people sinned more and more, God's wonderful kindness became more abundant. So just as sin ruled over all people and brought them to death, now God's wonderful kindness rules instead, giving us right standing with God and resulting in eternal life through Jesus Christ our Lord." (Rom 5:20–21 NLT).

What a marvelous, perplexing truth. God established fences and boundaries so He could show us that no matter how hard we try, we can not stay within them. We then realize that we need help, a Savior by whom His "wonderful kindness became more abundant."

One day, through the help of that Savior, life will be restored to how it was meant to be, and we will live in a better place, where: "No longer will there be any curse." (Rev 22:3 NIV). In the meantime there is a curse, people are born into poor families, and the innocent do die.

This is what I think. There comes a time God slams the door on our musings about life. If we insist, He will require us to stand to our feet and answer Him, much as he caused Job. There are things too great for us to wrap our finite minds around. There is God, and, there is Satan, it will be so till the end of time. Ultimately, however, the righteous are under God's hand: "The LORD does not let the righteous go hungry but he thwarts the craving of the wicked." (Prov 10:3 NIV).

Because Gideon was discouraged by his situation, his faith was crumbling, and he was placing God's faithfulness below his expectation of what he thought His faithfulness ought to be. Quite simply, you don't measure God by your understanding of life; you measure life by your understanding of God. In His Sovereignty rests all the unanswered questions, and, all the unquestioned answers. We can relate to Gideon's emotional response to the angel: "if the LORD is with us, why has all this happened to us?" We can relate to it because we too have had our emotions battered and our minds clouded by the discouragement we face in life. We have been told a lie that does not live up to our expectations. But, be reminded, blessing is not in having things in the land of many gods, it's in having God, in the land of many things.

#4 Discouragement leads to an unhealthy questioning of one's usefulness

"The LORD turned to him and said, 'Go in the strength you have and save Israel out of Midian's hand. Am I not sending you?' 'But Lord,' Gideon asked, 'how can I save Israel? My clan is the weakest in Manasseh, and I am the least in my family.'" (Ju 6.14-16).

The nation of Israel was composed of several units. Beginning with the nation itself, it was then divided by various tribes within the nation, various clans within the tribe, and finally to various families within the clan. Gideon's apprehension was that he of all people should be called of God to lead the nation against this massive enemy, Midian. In his estimation, he was the least of the least. That is, he felt the least in his family, which was the least in his clan, which was the least of the tribes in the little nation of Israel.

We've already seen that in his discouragement Gideon wasn't thinking of the faithfulness of a powerful God, who works in miraculous ways to accomplish great things through the weak. But, neither was he thinking very highly of himself. How could he, broken and weak, be the man God would call to save the entire nation of Israel? But, he was exactly in the position that God needed him in; left broken from the enemy's onslaughts, devoid of any sense of self-reliance, and spiritually melted down to know his dependence on his Creator.

Isn't it interesting how God responded to him: "go in this your strength," He said. Gideon's strength was his weakness, his dependency on God. The apostle Paul said something similar: "Therefore I take pleasure in infirmities, in reproaches, in needs, in persecutions, in distresses, for Christ's sake. For when I am weak, then I am strong." (2 Cor 12:10 NKJV). Weakness turned inward is death, but weakness turned upward is strength.

Some of the greatest sermons I've preached were born out of weakness. They were the times I felt spiritually insignificant, broken from personal casualty, or, burdened with the guilt of sinfulness. On my way to church, an emotionally bruised wife or child in tow, I knew I must step into the pulpit and deliver a message of help and healing to a waiting congregation. I would then kneel in surrender before God and remind Him that if He could use the stones to proclaim His truth, then I, as a vessel of unworthiness, would be willing to do the same.

Gideon was ready to be used of God. His "play dough" heart, hardened by the affairs of life, was being made soft again through the warming touch of God's massaging Hand. As God called on his service, he took a realistic look at his weaknesses, yet resolved to commit whatever he was or had to God's commission. God wants you to do the same in your tragic situations. As overwhelming as they may appear, God is greater.

In the "blessing" culture in which we live, dissatisfaction leads to discouragement, and discouragement denounces value; that is generally bad. Ironically, God takes bad and uses it for His good. In this case, a true look at one's worth leads to God's help. When we recognize that all mankind is weak and frail, He lifts us up to view a higher Source of help. It was not found within Gideon, the man. And, it is not found within us either. We need God's help to turn our disastrous affairs around. Maybe that's where you're at right now. God has been "nudging" you to do something about your situation. Maybe you sense He is calling you to take the lead for your "clan."

#5 Discouragement is overcome by faith

"The Lord answered, 'I will be with you, and you will strike down all the Midianites together.'" (Ju 6.16).

Those are the most comforting words for any battle weary warrior, God's promise that He "will be with you." When we cannot get past our own uselessness and mortality, it is by faith that we accept God's judgment of us. Gideon quit listening to his discourage-tainted view of himself, and by faith accepted God's call to get out of the winepress he was cowering in.

Gideon's musings over God's powerful and miraculous interventions became reality for him. He gathered thirty-two thousand men able to draw the sword and fight against the Midians, but God said to him, "…you have too many men for me to deliver Midian into their hands. In order that Israel may not boast against me that her own strength has saved her, announce now to the people, 'Anyone who trembles with fear may turn back and leave Mount Gilead.' So twenty two thousand men left, while ten thousand remained." (Judg 7:2-3 NIV).

But the odds were still too overwhelming for God, and He chiseled away again at the numbers of the army Gideon was marching with: "So Gideon took the men down to the water. There the Lord told him, 'Separate those who lap the water with their tongues like a dog from those who kneel down to drink.' Three hundred men lapped with their hands to their mouths. All the rest got down on their knees to drink. The LORD said to Gideon, 'With the three hundred men that lapped I will save you and give the Midianites into your hands. Let all the other men go, each to his own place.'" (Judg 7:5 7 NIV).

Let me interject a reminder here: the Midanites were so numerous they moved against Israel like swarms of locusts, and it was impossible to count their total, yet, God was rifling Gideon's ranks. Gideon was about to observe firsthand a miracle no less miraculous than those Gideon had been musing about in the winepress. Gideon's tiny army of three hundred blew their trumpets at God's appointed time: "When the three hundred trumpets sounded, the LORD caused the men throughout the [Midianite] camp to turn on each other with their swords. The army fled to Beth Shittah toward Zererah as far as the border of Abel Meholah near Tabbath." (Judg 7:22 NIV). What a tremendous word picture, the enemy turning against himself and fleeing from God's people in helter-skelter fashion.

That picture poses some interesting theology here, for God can do whatever He wants, including turning the enemy against himself, but he chooses to include people of faith in His mission. People of faith entrust both their lives and livelihood to the governance of the Creator, and not the "gods" of the land. People of faith are not distracted by their alluring surroundings. People of faith come to a pivotal point of belief, and choose God's assessment of them. People of faith are able to rest in the faithfulness of God. People of faith recognize their mortal weakness, yet know God's strength to overcome.

The slippery slope of wanting more suggests we need more than God offers, and leads many astray into indulgence. That is not God's best, and it is not His blessing. In hoping to indulge themselves in the "things" of the land they are living, they become steeped in the environment and "gods" surrounding them, thereby losing contact with the true "Treasure" of life.

Not only does the enemy rob them materially, but, he also robs them of joy, spiritual rest, and, financial contentment. That's the trade off, as the choice to gain independence from God is a choice to become yoked with the enemy. Jesus said, "Take my yoke upon you and learn from me, for I am gentle and humble in heart, and you will find rest for your souls. For my yoke is easy and my burden is light." (Mat 11:29 30 NIV).

I made a friend at a small church I was pastoring some years ago who was diagnosed with terminal cancer. Not having a church background, she welcomed the information I was sharing with her concerning her relationship with God. Her husband too had many questions, and one night we ended our conversation with prayer. I prayed with fervency and meaning, for I believed that much was at stake with the choices he was facing in his life. While my eyes were closed in concentration, his voice interrupted my prayer. "Stop now!" he said, "Don't pray for me any longer." Dismayed, I asked him why. "Because," he continued, "if I surrender my life to God, I will no longer have the impact I need with those who are working under me, and that will ruin my career!"

"Something" had convinced him that he would lose more than he would gain by surrendering his career to God. It is my conviction that he stands to lose more than a temporal career by his choice, for, the enemy leaves you naked and forlorn in the land. Discouraged and miserable, you may not even know why.

What starts out to be a mild diversion into the surrounding culture, ends up leaving us robbed of God's best. The enemy chisels away our hopes and takes from our hearts until we are a shambled heap of discouraged humanity. God shows us the way out, but His help requires no less than absolute surrender of our very lives to Him. That is, surrender of our resources, our morals, and our self-reliance. Full surrender requires us to give up our craving to be better off. Reflect on that last sentence a moment. What are we craving to be better off than? Dare we say better off than the greatest that God offers?

We have a choice, we can be content to follow the customs or our culture, or, we can discover a new contentment offered by God, but, we cannot have both: "…for either he will hate the one and love the other, or else he will be loyal to the one and despise the other. You cannot serve God and mammon." (Luke 16:13 NKJV).

I want to end with a last days warning that Jesus gave: "As it was in the days of Noah, so it will be at the coming of the Son of Man. For in the days before the flood, people were eating and drinking, marrying and giving in marriage, up to the day Noah entered the ark; and they knew nothing about what would happen until the flood came and took them all away. That is how it will be at the coming of the Son of Man." (Mat 24:37-39 NIV).

What seems to be the horrendous sin that was going on in the days of Noah? Was Jesus concerned over the conditions of the time, or was He concerned about the attitudes of the time? The conditions seem to be everyday conditions, benign really, including such things as eating, drinking, marrying, and giving in marriage. But, Jesus seems to be warning of something else here. His concern is with the attitude of the culture. It is an attitude so preoccupied with the everyday "things" of what this life offers that it neglects a fearsome day in which God will end all things suddenly and unexpectedly with a day of reckoning. "But the day of the Lord will come like a thief. The heavens will disappear with a roar; the elements will be destroyed by fire, and the earth and everything in it will be laid bare. Since everything will be destroyed in this way, what kind of people ought you to be? You ought to live holy and godly lives as you look forward to the day of God and speed its coming. That day will bring about the destruction of the heavens by fire, and the elements will melt in the heat. But in keeping with his promise we are looking forward to a new heaven and a new earth, the home of righteousness." (2 Pet 3:10-13 NIV).

The point is simple really. Do you remember watching the newscasts of the hurricane Katrina aftermath? People were on the roofs, dead bodies were floating in the foul water, alligators taken from abandoned pools, while snakes wandered dangerously close to the shelters where people had fled. In the chaos, hospitals were scurrying to evacuate heart, cancer, and other critical patients to safe and functioning facilities. People lost all they had materially. Their homes were totally obliterated by the powerful storm surge. The area was turned into miles of grayish rubble as viewed from the aerial shots of news stations. Cars had been effortlessly tossed around like toys, and personal possessions, which had been ripped out of residences by the constant barrage of wind, lay exposed before the eyes of the world. Everything was lost instantly.

They say in order to truly appreciate the devastation of that area you need to see it firsthand. My wife spent a few days in Waveland, Mississippi to help out a homeowner there. His home was spared because it was made of brick, all wood frame homes were torn apart. The water came about six miles inland. If you drew a mark on the wall of that home in Waveland, about five and one half feet up, you could eliminate salvaging anything from there down. As the water began to seep beneath the door they naively attempted to put a towel down to keep the moisture out. But in a flash the door burst open and the floodwaters surged through the home. They survived by climbing into the attic by a ladder. Their two dogs barely managed to survive. One was clinging to a cooler when rescued and he wouldn't let it go for three days after. The other dog, a lab, had tread water the entire time. When they finally reached him he held on to the rescuer for literally hours after.

The man in Waveland was two years away from retirement. He had built a business and was about to pass it along to his son. That day changed his plans forever. He lost his business and all his possessions in a matter of minutes. In his house everything was ruined except the hot water heater. He didn't live in a flood plain, no flood insurance was required there, and nobody ever expects a tragedy like that to ever hit them. The home insurance paid for a new roof, and that money was soon turned over to the bank to keep the mortgage up to date. After one year, they still live in the front yard, where three camping trailers are now considered "home."

Yet it is not those stories that pull at our heartstrings the most. "Things" can be rebuilt, or replaced, but, the man in Waveland lost his mother to the storm, and no benevolent groups would be able to replace her. And, who will ever forget the interview with the man whose family had been desperately fleeing floodwaters on the roof of their home? In that touching interview, where both the interviewed and the interviewer were moved to tears, the man told how he was unable to hold his wife as the house split apart and she began to float away. Her parting words to him were "take care of the children and the grandchildren." Life is more than "the toys that we die with!" That's Peter's point, and that's Jesus' last days warning! All the things of earth will be destroyed one day; they are really valueless, yet, in irony, they are what preoccupy much of our time.

In a dialogue with Franklin Graham of Samaritan's Purse, Diane Sawyer noted that the three things people taking refuge in the Superdome put on a list of most important items to have were "food, drink, and the Bible."[9] In the wake of hurricane Katrina, the people who lost loved ones do not need faith in what bankers promise and they do not need faith in the good intentions of politicians. Like those folks, maybe in some ways that's where you are, seemingly beaten and discouraged. But remember, as Gideon discovered, discouragement is overthrown by faith… faith in a God who loves you.

Be still my soul—Thy God doth undertake
To guide the future—As He has the past
Be still my soul—The waves and wind still know
His voice who ruled them—While He dwelt below[10]

"Blessing Means Having"

Small Group Discussion Questions
Chapter Three Review

1. How would discouragement be a pivotal point for either spiritual failure or success?

2. Does the statement: "Weakness turned inward is death, but weakness turned upward is strength," have special meaning for you? Explain you answer.

3. In what way are these modern times similar to the days of Noah? {cf. Mt. 24.37–39}

4. Did you watch the news concerning Hurricane Katrina? What stories moved you to tears or touched your heart? What life lessons do they leave us?

5. What event in your life would be your light at the end of the tunnel?

6. Has either having money or the lack of it ever become a spiritual distraction to you?

The Content and the Cravers— The Haves and the Have Nots

Here are some famous money quotes

Some are funny:

"Money can't buy you happiness but it does bring you a more pleasant form of misery." {Spike Milligan}

"Whoever said money can't buy happiness simply didn't know where to go shopping." {Bo Derek}

"Women prefer men who have something tender about them—especially legal tender." {Kay Ingram}

"I'm so naive about finances. Once when my mother mentioned an amount and I realized I didn't understand, she had to explain: 'That's like three Mercedes.' Then I understood." {Brooke Shields}

Some are thought provoking:

"Money isn't everything—but it's a long way ahead of what comes next." {Edmund Stockdale}

"When I was young I used to think that money was the most important thing in life. Now that I am old, I know it is." {Oscar Wilde}

"It isn't necessary to be rich and famous to be happy. It's only necessary to be rich." {Alan Alda}

"Somebody said to me, 'But the Beatles were anti-materialistic.' That's a huge myth. John and I literally used to sit down and say, 'Now, let's write a swimming pool.'" {Paul McCartney}

Some are just sad:

"...and now we're down to our last $37,000."
{Tammy Faye Bakker}

"I enjoy money. Not enough people in this world are happy. I'm determined to be contented, and having plenty of money from working makes it easier for me." {Karen Carpenter}[11]

When I was in elementary school, I heard a boy who lived in one of the more affluent homes around us say to my mother very kindly, "My mom and dad say you have no money, but, I say that you just probably don't choose to spend it on houses and cars and things you can see. Am I right?" In his young little innocent mind, he couldn't bear to know that some folks had to live the way we did. The world has always been made up of the haves and the have nots, but, it's a matter of our own choice as to whether we will be among the content or the cravers. That point was so important to God that He allowed it to be stressed in Scripture: "Let your character be free from the love of money, being content with what you have; for He Himself has said, "I will never desert you, nor will I ever forsake you." (Heb 13:5 NASB). It's all about the surrender of character to God, and not about the right to "captain our own soul," the former is based on contentment, whereas the latter is the fruit of craving.

Lot in the Old Testament is a good example of that. I suppose when we think of Lot we think of a rather non-spiritual man, but, Scripture seems to tell us otherwise:

> "…God rescued Lot out of Sodom because he was a good man who was sick of all the immorality and wickedness around him. Yes, he was a righteous man who was distressed by the wickedness he saw and heard day after day." (2 Pet 2:7 8 NLT).

Lot had traveled to Canaan with his childless uncle Abram. I surmise the two were very close, and possibly even had a father and son-like relationship. They were herdsmen and shared equal success with increasing their livestock. Because of this, the land could no longer support them together. When the quarreling started between the men of Abram and the men of Lot, we read that:

> "…Abram said to Lot, 'Let's not have any quarreling between you and me, or between your herdsmen and mine, for we are brothers. Is not the whole land before you? Let's part company. If you go to the left, I'll go to the right; if you go to the right, I'll go to the left.' Lot looked up and saw that the whole plain of the Jordan was well watered, like the garden of the Lord, like the land of Egypt, toward Zoar…So Lot chose for himself the whole plain of the Jordan …" (Gen 13:8 11 NIV).

Abram was a man contented with what God intended for his life, thus indicated by his decision to give Lot the first choice of where to go. Lot, on the other hand, looked around from his position and craved for the lush land of the Jordan valley near the towns of Sodom and Gomorrah. Lots craving led to his downfall, as indicated by three mistakes that he went through in making his decisions.

Mistake #1

We first see Lot making the decision to live near Sodom: "Abram lived in the land of Canaan, while Lot lived among the cities of the plain and pitched his tents near Sodom. Now the men of Sodom were wicked and were sinning greatly against the LORD." (Gen 13:12-13 NIV). In his mind, I'm sure Lot had made what he thought was the best decision for his future, but, his decision moved him among the cities of the Jordan, and Scripture says he "pitched his tents near Sodom," a place of wickedness and corruption.

I imagine that Lot could look out the flap of his tent and see the bustling town of Sodom. His tent was probably pointed in that direction. Maybe even the laughter from the revelry was carried to his ears by the nighttime winds, like the songs of the sirens. Perhaps the city lights glittering in the distance taunted his mind with suggestions of what he was missing. Whatever your take is on this, the point is, Lot craved for what he was seeing and hearing with his physical senses, and was not hearing from God.

There are times in my life that I pitch my "tent" too close to the temptation of what I hear and see with my physical senses, and not from God. On one such occasion, I was buying a television set. We had just left college, where life had been with few frivolities. Though we had a television, it was a little black and white version, but I had been dreaming of the day we could afford to buy a color one. About a year after we made it into the working community I had finally saved up enough money to buy that used color television I had been dreaming about.

With cash in hand, I entered into the used television repair shop that a friend had told me about. There it was! A little television not much bigger than the black and white one I had but beaming with such brilliant colors I could hardly keep my eyes off it. And, the price tag was exactly the amount that I had saved up. As far as I was concerned the decision was a no-brainer, I had the money, and, the television was precisely what I wanted. The craving that I had to purchase that little set was drowning out an inner "sense" that I shouldn't be in such a rush to buy.

Because the craving had been gnawing away for quite some time, I decided to go ahead and load the television into my car and bring it home that same day, ignoring the fact that it came with no warranty. I enjoyed the brilliant colors of that little set for about a week, when it abruptly ceased working. It was frustrating to hear the repairman as he announced the necessary repairs needed, and that it was going to take a good deal of money to get it working again. Even more frustrating was when a friend said to me, "I heard you just bought a color television, that's too bad, I had a nearly new one in my attic that I was going to give you." Using the vernacular of this chapter, I had pitched my tent too close to the craving of my physical senses, and it clouded my ability to hear from God, and to be satisfied with His best. That is exactly what happened to Lot.

Mistake #2

In time, the craving inside Lot brought erosion of his will. We don't know how much time had passed, but several surrounding nations gathered to make an attack on bountiful Sodom. Where was Lot in all this? In a striking passage, we learn he was no longer content to live on the plains facing Sodom, he eventually had moved into the city:

> "The victorious invaders then plundered Sodom and Gomorrah and began their long journey home, taking all the wealth and food with them. They also captured Lot, Abram's nephew who lived in Sodom, and took everything he owned." (Gen 14:11 12 NLT).

Mistake number two came when he opened his heart to the temptation. Having moved into the city, he no longer had to guess what the attraction was that he was hearing from his tent. The alluring city lights had now become his lights. But, in an instant, he lost all the wealth he had, and was held captive by the enemy.

There's an interesting spiritual lesson here. When we give ourselves over to our cravings, we eventually end up living in the midst of a spiritual enemy. Things will eventually be taken away. It seems we can never get ahead. If we earn more, we spend more. We move away from the protective care of God, becoming subject to depleted resources, as they are either wasted away, or stolen from us by unfortunate "incidents" that we fall prey to. The enemy is not loyal to his subjects. In Lot's case, the enemy took back as much as he had given, using an attack by the surrounding nations.

Thankfully, uncle Abram came to the rescue by saving Lot and recovering all the stolen goods that were lost to the invaders. The king of Sodom was prepared to give Abram bounty for his efforts, but, in a fascinating exposure of his character, Abram replied:

> "...I have solemnly promised the Lord, God Most High,

Creator of heaven and earth, that I will not take so much as a single thread or sandal thong from you. Otherwise you might say, 'I am the one who made Abram rich!'" (Gen 14:22 23 NLT).

There again we see the contrast between Abram and Lot. Abram did not care to be rich from what the King of Sodom offered, nor, was he about to allow the King to take credit for any measure of wealth he may obtain. He was not a craver, but was satisfied with God's care and provision for his life. And, Abram's character was unchanged by the titillating offer of bounty out of Sodom. Abram realized that the true source of gratification was staying content with God's provision.

Mistake #3

One might think that Lot would have learned a valuable lesson through his experiences, but, Lot remained in the wickedness of Sodom, even though his righteous soul was tormented, because his character was not free from the love of "things." In the end, he made the terrible choice to stay for the sake of economic security. That turned out to be his final, and most calamitous, mistake.

Apparently life for Lot was going well. He even had two lovely daughters that he had pledged in marriage to a couple of men from the city. As I said, things were good for all Lot knew. But, what Lot didn't know was that the immoral cries from that place had reached the ears of God. God had already decided to send two angels of destruction into the city. When the angels came, they mercifully asked Lot's family to leave before the destruction:

"With the coming of dawn, the angels urged Lot, saying,

'Hurry! Take your wife and your two daughters who are here, or you will be swept away when the city is punished.' When he hesitated, the men grasped his hand and the hands of his wife and of his two daughters and led them safely out of the city, for the LORD was merciful to them." (Gen 19:15-16 NIV).

I'm shocked to see how difficult it was for Lot to get out of the lifestyle he was living in. With pending doom on the horizon, and the angels warning that he would be "swept away" in destruction, he "hesitated" so that they grabbed his hand and pulled him out into safety. Jesus reminded us of "how hard it is for the rich to enter the kingdom of God!" (Luke 18:24 NIV).

On the day of destruction, when burning sulfur rained down out of the heavens upon that area, not only were the cities of Sodom and Gomorrah destroyed but also "...the entire plain, including all those living in the cities and also the vegetation in the land." (Gen 19:25 NIV). The once lush plains of vegetation that Lot had craved from the beginning were in the end ruined by the hand of God.

And how do we find Lot in the end? Was he happy? He was broken, leaving behind the once luscious plains he had desired, he settled instead in the mountains, hiding in a cave with his two daughters, having lost his wife to the lure of Sodom (cf. Gen 19). If you're listening to the "lie" concerning life's tomorrows, and are in the process of building bigger and better barns to hold all your "things," then you probably have a lot to worry about, because in the end, like Lot you will not be happy. As Jesus warned: "Do not lay up for yourselves treasures on earth, where moth and rust destroy and where thieves break in and steal; but lay up for yourselves treasures in heaven, where neither moth nor rust destroys and where thieves do not break in and steal." (Mat

6:19 20 NKJV). The "treasures of earth" will not last. By decay, destruction, or robbery, they will slowly be taken from us.

That is what my father tried to teach us, his children, by example. God's blessing was not in what he had materially, it was in knowing that the "king" of this world had not made him rich, and, that he thereby rested in the best that God offered. He was satisfied in the fact that God looked favorably upon His life, acting well toward him.

Make the time to take inventory of the things you hold precious to your heart. That one thing you hold most dearly will probably indicate if you bear the character of a "craver." Can you lose what you're holding? Only the things of God can never be lost.

The "lie" says to grab all the gusto that you can, and by any means you can, but cravers will always crave, because the world they live in cannot supply their wants. On the other hand, the Bible says there is an alternative. It is a life of trust, discipline, and honor. Trust in a Creator who knows all things, discipline to live within His realm of provision, and honor to live respectfully for Christ. You cannot choose to be born into the "haves" or the "have-nots", but you can choose to be content with God's provision for your life. Abraham was, and his decision was his blessing, for he pitched his tent in the direction of God's best.

"Blessing Means Having"

Small Group Discussion Questions
Chapter Four Review

1. Have you ever chosen your tent site based on your craving for physical desire or material goods?

2. How did Lot's love of things lead him to the day he had to be pulled out of Sodom?

3. Are you building "bigger and better barns" to hold your things?

4. Take some time to discuss what you believe to be most precious in your life.

5. Have you ever wanted relief from the pressure to "keep up with the Joneses?" If so, what or you doing about it? Does it include a budget cut?

6. Name some ways that you have contentment in your life. What, if anything, would eliminate that?

Section #2

The Second Lie: Morality Is Relative

Preface To Lie #2

The cover on a *Newsweek* magazine pictures a young lady standing with eyes closed. Her head is tilted back as if face to face with heaven, and her hands are raised in surrender before God. On the inside of the magazine is a news report entitled "In Search of the Spiritual." The article points out the historical "hunger" of people looking for a "deeper relationship with God." It states:

> "In sepulchral black and red, the cover of Time magazine dated April 8, 1966, Good Friday, introduced millions of readers to existential anguish with the question Is God Dead?…Nobody would write such an article now, in an era of round-the-clock televangelism and official presidential displays of Christian piety."[12]

The article suggests that what was born out of the sixties: "…in a cycle of renewal that has played itself out many times since the Temple of Solomon, was a passion for an immediate, transcendent experience of God. And a uniquely American acceptance of the amazingly diverse paths people have taken to find it."[13]

Strangely, this new diversity has also emerged into a culture of spiritual inclusiveness where folks are mixing and choosing from the various offers around them. As good as that sounds to some, the problem is one of absolutes. If there is no absolute there is no standard, and if there is no standard there is no morality, and if there is no morality there is no God, and coming full circle, if there is no God there is no absolute.

I really think what has evolved lately is an exhaustion of fighting all the political "battles." For example, many Christians point to what they view as hypocrisy in supporting a political agenda favoring "family values," when places like The Barna Group give the statistics that Christians are just as likely to get divorced as non-Christians.[14] It seems to me, the quest is for genuine spirituality, a personal "experience," and not an agenda. Younger America is less concerned over the "arenas" that have kept our political forefathers at each other. That sense of openness has allowed access to a flood of moral ambiguity. In some sense this new direction is comforting, for it seems to funnel the spiritual experience into what is genuinely real and personal for those that have an honest track on God. Yet, in another way it presents a plethora of problems, because it can lead to a re-definition of morality for those not having an honest track on God. As I already said, if there is no absolute there is no standard.

I like Barack Obama; he has this kind of morality by accident thing going for him. What I mean is that he comes to conclusions based on an internal "sense" of things. He doesn't claim to be a theologian or Bible scholar, but he has really impressed me by this innate awareness of fairness and good judgment. If nothing else, he's real.

Ironically, it is his own assessment to the discovery of his "inner" truth that concerns me. It leads to the previously mentioned re-definition of morality to those not having a real track on God. He states: "For those who believe in the inerrancy of the Bible, as many evangelicals do, such rules of engagement may seem just one more example of the tyranny of the secular and material worlds over the sacred and eternal. But in a pluralistic democracy, we have no choice. Almost by definition, faith and reason operate in different domains and involve different paths to discerning truth."[15]

In a further explanation of that, he uses the illustration of Abraham and Isaac, concluding with: "And yet it is fair to say that if any of us saw a 21st century Abraham raising the knife on the roof of his apartment building, we would call the police; we would wrestle him down; even if we saw him lower the knife at the last minute, we would expect the Department of Children and Family Services to take Isaac away and charge Abraham with child abuse. We would do so because God doesn't reveal Himself or His angels to all of us in a single moment. We do not hear what Abraham hears, do not see what Abraham sees, true as those experiences may be. So the best we can do is act in accordance with those things that are possible for all of us to know, understanding that a part of what we know to be true-as individuals or communities of faith-will be true for us alone." This is not to say that I'm unanchored in my faith. There are some things that I'm absolutely sure about-the Golden Rule, the need to battle cruelty in all its forms, the value of love and charity, humility and grace."[16]

It seems to me that an important factor needs to be considered in the mix of moral relevance. We need to ask the question: "What is your moral compass based on?" What's interesting to me, is that the things Barack Obama is sure of, such as the Golden Rule, are things that the moral compass within him is designed to point "north" about. At some point in his life, he enabled the moral compass to operate by opening his heart up to God.

When you open your heart up to God the "spirit of the law," and not just the "letter of the law," becomes real to us. It is not a matter of personal opinion or individual judgment, it is a standard based on God's Word and our inner compass. That moral compass seems to be generally approved by society. We put people in jail for stealing, cheating, or killing others. Those are laws based on a standard of ancient written codes that are interpreted by the inner moral code.

But even the less obvious moral truths are based on a deeper sense of understanding when held up to the light of God's righteousness. For example, the ancient code reads: "Remember the sabbath day, to keep it holy." (Exo 20:8 NASB). That was interpreted by the authorities of the day in the "letter of the law" to mean that literally nothing was to be done on the Sabbath Day. But Jesus once healed a man on the Sabbath Day, causing a great commotion to which He responded: "…If one of you has a son or an ox that falls into a well on the Sabbath day, will you not immediately pull him out?" (Luke 14:5 NIV). And why did He respond with that? Because He knew in the "spirit of the law" that: "…The Sabbath was made for man, not man for the Sabbath." (Mark 2:27 NIV). Jesus honored the holiness of God and obeyed the "letter of the law," as He likewise honored the righteousness of God as He obeyed the "spirit of the law." God's righteousness is based on His holiness.

Going back to the Abraham and Isaac illustration, my conviction is that the decision Abraham made was a right decision for anybody to make. The letter of the law was saying "thou shall not kill," but the spirit of the law was asking for blind obedience to what he could not immediately understand. But what he did understand was the promise that his seed through Isaac would increase, and that even if Isaac died: "Abraham reasoned that God could raise the dead ..." (Heb 11:19 NIV). In this case, as in all cases, faith and reason operated together.

When Barak Obama says that faith and reason do not operate together, it hints at an implication that I'm uneasy about, that morality is relative to the individual it involves, the circumstance he is in, or the time he is in it. If that opinion is held by someone who holds no accountability to God, the results are truly catastrophic. It leads to a re-definition of morality, one based on something other than the standard established by God which has been placed into our moral compass.

Have you ever tweaked a recipe? I do it all the time. Just a few months ago my son called to tell me he and his wife were coming by. It was about suppertime, so I suggested that we eat together. That was a good idea, he thought, and asked if I would try out this new recipe he had for chicken.

I agreed, and he gave me the ingredients and baking directions. As I looked it over, I decided the recipe would taste better if a specific ingredient was exchanged for another. And, I also decided to add one ingredient that he had not mentioned at all. By the time they arrived, the dish they had been hoping for was entirely different than the one I served.

Everything we know tells us that you cannot indiscriminately change the recipe and expect the same results. Yet, that is exactly what we do with God. We tweak His moral "recipe" and have results that leave us sadly disappointed and without an acceptable standard for living. In the next few chapters, I want to give a voice to the need for a decent standard of morality.

Brittle Standards

Recently, certain laws we have held over the years have been challenged as to their constitutional compliance. The real concern for me is not over the changing of laws, it is over shifting morality. You do not control morality by laws, you control laws by morality. When you change the standard for morality, the laws are not far behind.

Our beliefs embrace a standard for the truth we choose to live by. The US government has established a standard for product truth, by which all businesses within our boundaries are held to. It is the standard for weights and measurements. That is why all contractors build using a standard way of measuring one foot, or, all grocery stores weigh out a pound by using scales periodically checked to be sure they conform to required standard. If not, supposedly similar buildings would have vastly different dimensions, and the weighted items you brought home would vary from store to store. Anything that does not fit within the government's standards is rejected as a misrepresentation of truth, and punishable by severe fines or penalties.

Moral truth has a standard of measurement as well. It is a way by which all other concepts of morality can be measured, weighed, and finally either accepted as truth, or rejected as misrepresentation. But whose truth should we follow, and whose truth is real truth? I believe the God of the Bible is not fearful of challenge. Test Him with an open heart. Challenge Him to show you absolute truth. But only stand before Him if your challenge is sincere and your heart is prepared to listen.

There are certain truths of God that we simply know internally. And why do we know them? Because God has made us to know them:

> "...since what may be known about God is plain to them, because God has made it plain to them. For since the creation of the world God's invisible qualities—his eternal power and divine nature—have been clearly seen, being understood from what has been made, so that men are without excuse. (Rom 1:19–20 NIV).

Look at the marvel of creation around you. Look at the marvel of your own existence. While scientists have used "life" to spark life, they have never been able to create the "germ" of life. Consider your DNA:

> DNA contains about 2,000 genes per chromosome
> 1.8 meters of dna are folded into each cell nucleus
> A nucleus is 6 microns long

> "This is like putting 30 miles of fishing line into a cherry pit. And it isn't simply stuffed in. It is folded in. If folded one way, the cell becomes a skin cell. If another way, a liver cell, and so forth. To write out the information in one cell would take 300 volumes, each volume 500 pages thick. The human body contains enough dna that if it were stretched out, it would circle the sun 260 times."[17]

The invisible attributes of God, while invisible to the human eye, are visible in our "knower," being clearly seen through His creation. It is to that "knower" within you that I appeal, as we turn to the one Creator God of the universe for a truth standard. Without truth there could be no reality, for reality needs to be based on truth. It is by God's moral code of truth that we must operate if we are to have any reality to morality. Consider the following three things about morality:

1. It is obvious that people follow a different set of moral standards than God does.

   People are often not very tender or loving towards one another. A good friend of mine told me a story that illustrates the point. She was visiting her doctor in the bustling little office near where she lived. A woman was sitting in the waiting room near her who had gotten her attention. The woman was clearly in need of seeing a doctor, as she was coughing continually, grimacing in pain.

   Both the woman and my friend were called out of the waiting room at the same time. Together they left, ushered into individual examination rooms, where they waited for the doctor. The two private rooms were adjacent to one another, and my friend could easily hear the conversation going on next door.

   The woman had already undressed, put on a gown, and was waiting for the doctor's arrival. In the meantime, someone discovered that this woman's paperwork was incomplete, so a nurse was sent to fill in the necessary details. The conversation went something like this: "I don't see that any insurance company is named on your form, how are you going to pay for this visit?" The woman paused for some time, and then admitted she had neither medical insurance nor the cash on hand to pay for the visit. "Well," the nurse stated sternly, "You better put your clothes back on. When you get the money you can come back and see the doctor."

My friend, remembering the grimacing pain that this woman was in, was horrified by what she had heard. She said she had offered to pay for this woman's visit, but was not permitted to do so because: "patients were expected to work out their own medical plans." Apparently that was the standard in that office in regards to payment, and it was not likely to bend very easily.

The problem is, rigid standards are also brittle, and, though they don't bend, they often break at critical junctures. Consequently, those standards change according to feeling, pressures of life, or the whim of the standard maker. That is why a man's handshake is no longer his word, neither for that matter is his signature on a piece of paper. Brittle standards are broken all the time, whether they are contracts of marriage, employment, or the borrowing of money.

2. God's standards, though firm, are cloaked in mercy.

God asks that a certain relationship exist among His creation. That is precisely why the Ten Commandments were given. They are, in essence, the decent way to treat a fellow human being and the proper respect to be given God. Jesus summed all of the Ten Commandments up in a few words, saying:

"You shall love the Lord your God with all your heart, with all your soul, and with all your mind. This is the first and great commandment. And the second is like it: You shall love your neighbor as yourself. On these two commandments hang all the Law and the Prophets." (Mat 22:37 -40 NKJV).

I'll never know what it's like to raise a little girl, as my wife and I ended our child bearing after having three boys. Our boys were definitely boys! On one occasion we were having the church family over the house for a special event. I wasn't aware that one of our boys, around four years old at the time, was acting out of control. He had been spoken to several times by my wife, who figured it was now at the point where I needed to step in.

As I walked into the situation, I could see the defiant look on that little boy's face. I took him by the arm, howling and wailing loudly, away from the crowded room to his bedroom upstairs. I was absolutely determined to spank him soundly. I could feel the anger welling up inside me as he challenged my authority, embarrassing me in front of the church family. As I plopped him down on the bed, I prepared to do what I knew had to be done.

I managed to pause for a moment in my spirit, trying to gather my composure. It was in that moment of pause I distinctively heard God's gentle voice speak to my heart. "Show him mercy!" Show him mercy? I doubted it was really God instructing to do that. This child deserved a good spanking. But, I attentively paused again. "Show him mercy! Use this time to teach him of My love for him, as you have felt My love and mercy for you."

I sat on one side of the bed, and he was sitting on the other. That young man was hard in his determination to be set against me, his mom, and the world around him! He was not broken, tearful, fearful, or in the least bit repentant. I remember that it was almost frightening for me to see. I had seen steely eyed criminals with the same determination. I didn't know what to do, so I did what I believed God told me to do.

I pulled his stiffened body over to me, as he pushed away in insolence. I held him close to my chest and began to explain how I was about to give him a spanking, that he deserved a spanking, but, that God wanted me to give him love this time. I could feel the tenseness in his little body start to relax as I continued. I explained that there are times that I need to feel love too, that there were times in my life that I too had deliberately disobeyed God, and, that it was in those times that God pulled me close to His chest.

As I talked about God's love and mercy that little guy began to weep bitterly. If anyone had been listening in, they would have assumed I had beaten him severely. But, I was not the one meeting out discipline this time; it was God doing surgery on my little boy's heart. When he wept, then I wept. We both clung to each other madly, warm tears streaming uncontrollably down our cheeks. Nearly collapsing in emotion, we then prayed together for God's forgiveness in his life, and thanked Him for being a God of love and mercy.

He left that room a changed little boy, as evidenced by his excellent behavior for the rest of the night. There were ongoing occasions for the proper meting out of spankings, but on that occurrence, God wanted to teach us both about mercy. I have been reminded many such times since, that God's standards, though firm, are indeed cloaked in mercy to the repentant. I am so glad that I am not judged by human standards.

3. People understand right from wrong, but refuse to hear the truth of it.

For some reason, people have adopted brittle, self serving standards of morality, while the stinging truth about God is hidden behind closed hearts: "For the wrath of God is revealed from heaven against all ungodliness and unrighteousness of men, who suppress the truth in unrighteousness …" (Rom 1:18 NKJV).

I'll never forget the time my mother-in-law visited us while we were in college. We lived in a tiny apartment on campus, and, frankly, it was difficult to keep up with housework with my wife working full-time while I was attending classes and watching our newborn son. Occasionally dishes and pans piled up and overflowed the sink.

My mother-in-law was a good housekeeper, with things generally tidy and in place at her home. Our place was an absolute mess when my wife and I saw the car pull up outside. Facing each other in horror, we began scurrying around to tidy up whatever we could at the last minute. Suddenly my wife had an idea. "We don't have time," she said, "Let's pack up everything we can into the oven and close the door!" And that's just what we did, dirty dishes and pans, along with anything that had no immediate place to go ended up in the oven behind a closed door.

When my mother-in-law entered, we greeted her warmly with hugs and kisses. Once settled in, she proudly took the wrapping off the casserole she had brought along on her three-hour trip to our house. "I've brought dinner with me," she said, "All we have to do is warm it up in the oven."

The truth about our messy apartment was revealed when the oven door came open, it was a sudden "truth connection" that we could not deny. It is that truth connection with God that people with a moral appetite crave, and it is that craving that God satisfies through His written mandate of moral laws. The "oven door" is thrown open, revealing our dirty lives, and forcing us into either confession or excuse.

Those clinging to brittle standards hold a hollow view towards money, or morality, or responsibility, or whatever humanity uses to set the measurement for happiness, peacefulness, satisfaction, or success. You can try to hide God's moral truth in the denial "oven", but what do you do when the surprise "visit" comes? What do you do when the Dr.'s office calls with devastating test results? What do you do when an accident claims the life of your son or daughter? How do you handle infidelity?

In my personal experience, the further I closed the door on God's moral truths, the more difficult it became to recognize the brittle standards by which I lived. It's like the story I read some time ago about a little girl named Janie. She was about to become a big sister, as her expectant mom had gone to the hospital.

Shortly thereafter, the baby boy was born, and Janie got to ride next to him on the trip home, taking in his every move and sound. A few days had passed when Janie approached her mom and dad with a question, "Can you let me go see baby brother in his room by myself?" she asked. Mom and dad were a little nervous about Janie's motives, thinking she might be jealous over the little one who was now demanding so much attention, so they brushed her question aside. But Janie was persistent over the next several days as mom and dad considered her request carefully. They finally agreed to let Janie visit her baby brother alone in his nursery, but they would leave the door cracked open just a bit, to observe from a distance.

Little Janie was delighted when mom and dad let her go into baby brother's room alone. She slowly walked over to his crib, being cautious not to disturb him too abruptly. Then, she ran her little fingers through his hair, pulled down his blanket and counted all his fingers and toes. With the innocence of a three year old, she asked her baby brother the pounding question that she had for so long been holding in, "Baby brother," she said, "Could you remind me what God is like, I'm starting to forget!"

In the same way, the further we wander from God's standards of morality, closing the door of our hearts to them, the more difficult it becomes to recognize what His truth really is, and what God is really like. God is merciful, loving, and forgiving. He is unlike what the woman discovered in the Dr.'s office. For while God's moral standards are immovable, they are soaked in His mercy and forgiveness: "For what the Law could not do, weak as it was through the flesh, God did: sending His own Son in the likeness of sinful flesh and as an offering for sin …" (Rom 8:3 NASB).

For me, embracing God's moral standards emancipated me from the bowels of the lie. Truth is truth, and eventually the suppressed morality I had been living with came forth to expose the instability and frailty of the brittle standards that I had adopted. Again, I am reminded of my father's stability, which was formed from dedication to the pure standards of moral truth. As a young man, when I forced myself to look hard into the mirror, I was tired of the lie I was telling myself, and I hungered to live by the same standards as my father. God's morality is the standard by which all other "truth" is measured and weighed, my spiritual definition now begins with that fact, and, it is a premise from which I will not wander nor be moved.

Brittle standards eventually break, and leave the disappointed follower in ruins. My wife worked at a bank as a teller at the time of this writing. She was robbed the night before I wrote this. I went to see her as shortly after work as I could. The FBI, detectives, and local police units were still there taking down information and getting any crime scene evidence. I had parked in view of the front door in hopes that my wife would see my vehicle and come to let me know she was all right. A local police officer noticed me instead, and assured me that my wife was shaken, but uninjured. He told me it would be just a few minutes more, as they had the suspect in custody and on his way there to be identified by my wife and her co-worker.

I moved my vehicle away from the front door and waited along the side of the bank. Internally, I was mulling over the fact that the criminal who had just threatened my vulnerable wife was about to be brought within a few feet from where I was waiting. My wife had already been through this in a prior incident, a few months before, where the robber held a loaded gun just a few inches from her head and demanded in obscene language that she empty her money into a sack. I was tired of this for the sake of my wife. I knew how shaken she had been the last time it happened, and was thinking what I would like to say, or even do, to this assaulter of my wife's dignity if given the chance.

The police cruiser drove up with the suspect riding in the front seat. As they arrived at the front door of the bank, an officer approached the passenger side of the car, shining a light into the suspect's face. My wife and co-worker identified him from inside the bank, and, he was carted off to be processed as an armed robber.

In the meantime, I was going through a paradigm shift of emotions. I too had gotten a good look at the suspect, who was not bearing the hardened criminal look I was expecting. My anger turned to sorrow and pity for this wretched out of luck stranger who had made a choice that was about to ruin his life. He looked much like one's next door neighbor, or even friend. I saw a man sitting in the front seat of that cruiser that reminded me of a treed raccoon trying to escape the horror of the barking dogs at the base of the tree. A frail man with desperate eyes, he looked disoriented, like trying to awaken from a very bad dream that he would never wake from. He may never get to see the children who were with him in the getaway car graduate from school, or play baseball with them in the backyard, or walk down the aisle to give them away in marriage.

What a terrible choice he made, to trust in his own misconception of truth, a belief system he followed that convinced him that he could get away with bank robbery, and, that somehow the answer to his problems could be solved with the money he would gain from that. That's the point of this chapter. Some hold to a belief system that undermines and "buries" the moral codes of God, exchanging them for what the world offers to replace them with. The problem is that God's moral codes keep surfacing through our conscience. Our choice is to bury them in life's "oven," convincing ourselves that we will get away with keeping them out of "sight," or, we can surrender to the higher standard of morality that lay within us.

A man, in the end, will never be honored for what he is in the flesh. In the end, he will not be valued for his money, muscle, or magnitude. Those things simply will not last, and will bit by bit return to the dust they came from. All man's dust looks the same in the end, but a man's character, that is the great divide among us. That is in the end what separates one man from another. That's what is eternal and true. This is what my father taught me about having brittle standards, that they do not last in the end.

"Morality is Relative"

Small Group Discussion Questions
Chapter Five Review

1. Have standards changed in society within the last several years? Discuss how the general population views morality today verses years ago.

2. Why are people unwilling to accept a standard of right and wrong in their personal lives?

3. In what ways are the moral standards of our culture hypocritical? Discuss why they are not able to stand up to God's standards.

4. Does believing in a moral Creator affect your standards differently than atheist's standards might affect them? Why or why not?

5. How does God's standard of justice relate to His mercy? Have you ever experienced mercy from someone you had wronged or didn't deserve it from?

6. Have you ever intentionally shut out what God was saying so you wouldn't "see it" in your heart? (cf. Rom. 1: 18–19).

Our Source of Life

My youngest son was visiting some friends down the street when he was around fifteen or sixteen years old. They were a family that had four very attractive girls whose ages ranged somewhere around his. Part of the family was a very large dog named Samson, a black Labrador retriever that looked like he had been taking steroids. My son was standing next to the back screen door holding Samson by a leash, waiting to take him outside for a walk.

Obviously distracted, my son was paying attention to the girls talking to him. Samson, on the other hand, was himself distracted by something on the other side of the screen door. With a sudden burst of power and energy, Samson exploded through the screen door and down the stairs to chase after whatever it was he saw. Unfortunately, my son was still holding on to the leash. With a jarring slam he was pulled through the screen door and dragged down the stairs to the backyard, finally stopping at Samson's mercy. Dazed by the head slam into the door, he checked for injuries over various parts of his body.

The point is, he was strapped to an object that he was paying little attention to. Distracted by the pretty little girls and friendly conversation, he got sidetracked. The object he was strapped to was powerful and had a mind of its own. Because he wasn't paying attention, it hauled him dangerously close to real injury. Spiritually, if you're not paying attention, the distracting, powerful things of this world will take you where you don't want to go. The consequences are even more severe to us spiritually than the consequences that were to my son physically. We must pay attention to our moral lives. Giving in to even the slightest distraction could land us in the "backyard" of this world. Dazed and bruised, we will not even realize how we got there.

You can't have a proper foundation for morality without understanding what it essentially means. Morality, as described in the *New Century Dictionary,* is the quality, or character, which we bring into the act of conforming to that which is right conduct.[18] In chapter five I discussed the standards for establishing right conduct, and, in this chapter, I want to talk about the source of our character. The source of our character generates the life that enables our direction of conduct. Put simply, without a source of life, we have no moral compass.

Several years ago we planted a peach tree in our back yard, a gift from a loving church family that we were serving. We watched as she struggled for survival, hanging her branches in the scorching heat, and unable to bear fruit. Why was she having such a hard time? She was planted out in the open with no protection, daily feeling the exposure to the sun, wind, and other elements of nature that she was unaccustomed to. To further complicate her chances of survival, she was placed in an area of the yard where the water hose could not reach. Being from New England, my wife and I soon learned a valuable lesson about planting vegetation in the warm climate of the south, that is, without a water source things are cursed to die!

The Bible paints a similar picture of those who put their

trust in humanity. Because they do not have God as their source for life, they are cursed to wither and die: "This is what the LORD says: 'Cursed is the one who trusts in man, who depends on flesh for his strength and whose heart turns away from the LORD. He will be like a bush in the wastelands; he will not see prosperity when it comes. He will dwell in the parched places of the desert, in a salt land where no one lives.'" (Jer 17:5, 6 NIV).

In our minds we embrace that truth, but in our hearts we fall victim to the "lie." We inwardly listen to the non-Biblical principle of "The Lord helps those who help themselves." It's easy to do that, as that is the pattern humanity has followed from his days in the garden of Eden: "And the LORD God commanded the man, saying, 'Of every tree of the garden you may freely eat; but of the tree of the knowledge of good and evil you shall not eat, for in the day that you eat of it you shall surely die.'" (Gen 2:16 17 NKJV). "Then the serpent said to the woman, 'You will not surely die. For God knows that in the day you eat of it your eyes will be opened, and you will be like God, knowing good and evil.'" (Gen 3:4 5 NKJV). The lie was introduced and accepted, that people could be their own gods, and, therefore, disregard any higher authority source for life's direction. But, the point Jeremiah makes in the prior Scripture quoted, is crucial in understanding why we are forever striving towards a moral compass. That is, mortal flesh is no source for spiritual life, and therefore, cannot give moral direction.

The hope for a man's cure physically, emotionally, financially, and spiritually does not ultimately rest upon one's doctor, employer, or any other source of supposed help that this life can offer. Hope is an extension of knowing and trusting that God is sovereign, and in control of your current state in the world. That is the beginning of wisdom, a breaking away from the lie, and a step towards God's truth.

I believe that when you're serious with your commitment to trust God fully with your life, there comes a time when the world of flesh and the world of the spiritual will be in contention for your attention. A Biblical example of that is found in the gospel of Matthew.

After the hideous murder of his cousin John, via beheading, Jesus went off by boat for a solitary time of reflection. When he landed, a crowd had gathered, and, as usual, Jesus ministered to the sick and needy. As evening approached, and there was no nearby village to get food, Jesus told His disciples to feed them. At least five thousand folks were miraculously fed that night with five loaves of bread and a couple of fish as a display brought on by Christ's great compassion for people. [cf. Mt 14:1-21].

When evening set in, Jesus sent the apostles away by boat across the Galilean Sea, letting them know that He would catch up with them later. While the boat was some distance from shore, a windstorm settled in and challenged their ability to row to the other side against the heavy waves. Imagine being there that night with the apostles. Darkness surrounds you in its blanket, and you know you're in a deadly, watery grave-like environment. The angry sea douses you every time the boat is tossed by another vicious wave. It's around 3 o'clock in the morning and you're beginning to wear from the physical and emotional stress of trying to survive the night. Suddenly, and out of nowhere, a figure approaches from a distance, and, it's walking on the water!

Scripture says these men: "...were terrified. 'It's a ghost,' they said, and cried out in fear.'" (Mat 14:26 NIV). A strangely familiar voice then careened across the open water: "Take courage! It is I. Don't be afraid." (Mat 14:27 NIV). The voice was recognized as that of Jesus, but they pondered if it could be truly Him. This was a moment when their world of flesh collided with the spiritual. Even though they had witnessed the miraculous feeding of five thousand just a few hours earlier, their weakened states could not justify that a man could walk on water! They had never seen Jesus in this light, or perspective, for never before had their own lives been so destitute and frail. It had always been someone else's need, someone else's disease or fear, but now it was theirs!

There have been many times in my life that Jesus challenged my fleshly world of doubts and fears with the spiritual. I interned under a wonderful man of God who mentored me through a period of my life that solidified some loose-ended spiritual dimensions for me. On one occasion, he invited me to sit in on a counseling session, forewarning me that the subject matter was to be very intense. I had read about demonic oppression in the Bible, and knew that foreign mission fields dealt with these problems from time to time, but up until that point had never come face to face with the demonic.

The young lady sat directly across from me on a piano bench. She was barely out of high school, with long blonde hair. I had heard she had tampered with witchcraft and the occult during her school days, and silently wondered how such a young life could have been led so far astray. Her spiritual torment was obvious and showing through her movements.

The pastor broke into my silent contemplation with an urgent appeal to pray. I lowered my head, but hundreds of thoughts pummeled my brain and stifled my prayer. I was pondering what I was doing there, why I had chosen to come, when in a sudden fury the pastor commanded the spirit tormenting the young girl to leave. It has been over 30 years ago now, but I can still quote the verbal response made by that spirit.

In an instant I rose from my seat and rushed out the door. Pacing the hallway some distance from that room, I was reflecting on what I had just seen and heard. I felt frightened, confused, amazed, and disturbed by it all. Yet, I knew that this young girl was in desperate need of healing. My head was comfortable to believe that these things occurred in the Bible, or on foreign soil, but, now I was seeing it in another light, and from another perspective, it was now in my world.

As I continued to pace, God dared my heart concerning truth and faith. The pastor's wife, "by chance," came towards me in the hallway. "What's going on," she asked. Humbly before her I confessed the fear that I so needed to communicate. In gentle, yet strikingly profound words, God used her to challenge the core of my faith, reminding me that as a Christian I had no reason to question God's shield of protection in my life.

I made a decision in that moment that was a spiritual turning point with deep ramifications for me. The theology in my head, planted there through several years of training under the absolute finest Biblical scholars that any school could muster, had to travel the difficult journey from my head to my heart. In brokenness I acknowledged my fear and lack of faith before God, asked for His protection, and vowed to myself that it was better to die than to live a lifetime of spiritual doubt and lie.

Re-entering the room that the counseling "process" was taking place in, I was just in time to witness a miraculous and powerful deliverance for this girl, out of her bondage of demonic oppression, into the hands of a healing Savior. I don't know where that girl is today, or if she remains out of bondage, but I do know that God touched her life that day, along with mine, as He broke through to challenge my world with His spiritual world.

It was Peter who called out his doubts to the Lord in the boat that night: "Lord... if it's you... tell me to come to you on the water." (Mat 14:28 NIV). You can sense a certain determination in Peter's request, as if it was a do or die proposition. If it is Jesus, He will save us, and if it isn't, well, we're going to die here anyway.

I can envision Peter grabbing the side of the boat with his tough and weathered fisherman hands, hoisting himself up and over the edge onto the water. He probably never took the time to test if the water supported his weight, just up and over he flew. And miraculously, to his delight, the water supported his body. It was not enough that Peter had witnessed Jesus feed five thousand on five loaves of bread and a couple of fish, this was Peter's time for a personal encounter between his world of flesh and the spiritual world.

In the moments that followed, something enigmatic occurred within Peter. The closer he moved towards Jesus, the more he slipped under the waves of the sea. Nothing externally had changed. The storm didn't change, the situation in the boat hadn't changed, and Jesus didn't change. It was something inside Peter that changed. He began to doubt, and reached up desperately to his Lord: "... he was afraid and, beginning to sink, cried out, 'Lord, save me!' Immediately Jesus reached out his hand and caught him. 'You of little faith,' he said, 'why did you doubt?'" (Mat 14:30 31 NIV).

The point is that one's source of life does not come from within his capacities and strengths. It was not within Peter on the raging sea, it was not within me behind the closed doors where demons spoke, and it is not within you either when you are suddenly faced with horrific news. We wither, die, and sink when we try to depend on ourselves. It is all about emptying all we have, all of ourselves, into the fullness of God, to do or die.

There are times in your life where you ought to experience Jesus as more than a friend, and, even more than the Savior. It is not hard for God to bring us into His Kingdom. He can just speak the word and we'll cease to breathe. But, bringing heaven into us is a lifelong process. Remember, Jesus taught us to pray: "…May your will be done here on earth, just as it is in heaven." (Mat 6:10 NLT).

There are times He ought to challenge your world of flesh with His world, and carve into your life a set of truths that cannot be discovered in any way apart from a personal confrontation with the miraculous. He is Lord over all things, the source of life! That is the discovery of truth not found in a classroom, or between the covers of a book, it is the tuning of your soul to discover God's reality. It is a ringing in one's being that starts the migration of fact from one's mind, to one's very spirit.

The lie says that the source of life is from within us. It says that we are capable of rational thinking, that we are "the captain of our own souls", and that all we need to do is "follow our hearts." But that lie stands in direct contradiction of God's truth. "The heart is deceitful above all things and beyond cure. Who can understand it?" (Jer 17:9 NIV). Building the foundation of your life by "following your heart" is like building a house on ice. When the heat is on, it will all melt down beneath you.

Like the little peach tree planted in the scorching weather, we cannot stand alone in this difficult world environment. We need a source of life, or we will wither and die! Again, I am grateful for my father. I watched a man planted in the most difficult of surroundings flourish under the hand of his God. He never seemed to make it by the standards of the world. He left my mother with nothing tangible when he passed, save the mortgaged roof of an older home in need of repair. But, he also left us who knew him an example of successful living, that is, of placing your roots in the fertile ground that lies upon the banks of God's spiritual river. That is a place of healing, strength, and peaceful satisfaction, for the source of life there is immense, it never fails or disappoints.

My father trusted God with the most important things in his life, and I know that I too must follow that principal and pass it along to a third generation. I am reminded of that in everyday life. As I sat watching the pre-game show for Super bowl XXXVIII they highlighted a few of the most successful quarterbacks the game of football has ever had, namely, Jim Kelly, Boomer Esiason, Dan Marino, and Trent Dilfer. These outstanding athletes all had children who were assailed by a malady in their young lives. Boomer and Jim still struggle with the daily threat of losing their sons, Trent recently lost his five year old son to a rare and fatal heart disease, and Dan is still being the encouraging father to a young man troubled by autism. Their stories are heart-rending, and have left the four tremendous quarterbacks with similar mandates for anyone who will listen. The most important things in life are not career, income, or famous names, but holding that loved one close to the heart, and, dousing them with showers of kisses and encouraging words, filling their soul with unforgettable memories to combat sadder days that may loom upon the horizon. Strength for that comes from a source beyond the four walls of a gym at training camp. We must entrust the most precious things we have to be watered from a loving spring of God's ever flowing well.

In Genesis, the Bible tells the story of Abraham and Sarah. Both had wanted children passionately, yet, Sarah's womb had been dry for over ninety years. In a miraculous turn of events, God told Sarah that she soon would be pregnant with a boy child. Abraham must have been ecstatic when Sarah, the love of his life for nearly a century, finally gave birth to a baby, the product of two lives who had long passed their prime for having children. Finally, a rightful heir to his hard earned legacy, a son he could teach, the inheritor of his values. Isaac, as the boy was named, was the object of his affection.

Imagine his dismay, when with a command to test Abraham's trust, God ordered him to sacrifice Isaac, the "promise" of his patient waiting. The reading in Genesis chapter 22 is amazing to follow:

> "So Abraham rose early in the morning and saddled his donkey, and took two of his young men with him, and Isaac his son; and he split the wood for the burnt offering, and arose and went to the place of which God had told him. Then on the third day Abraham lifted his eyes and saw the place afar off. And Abraham said to his young men, 'Stay here with the donkey; the lad and I will go yonder and worship, and we will come back to you.'" (Gen 22:3 5 NKJV).

One of two things happened here: either Abraham chose to lie to the two young servants with him, or, he believed with all his heart that both he and his son would be coming back after worshipping God. I believe the latter is correct, and substantiated by the following verses:

"So Abraham took the wood of the burnt offering and laid it on Isaac his son; and he took the fire in his hand, and a knife, and the two of them went together. But Isaac spoke to Abraham his father and said, 'My father!' And he said, 'Here I am, my son.' Then he said, 'Look, the fire and the wood, but where is the lamb for a burnt offering?' And Abraham said, 'My son, God will provide for Himself the lamb for a burnt offering.' So the two of them went together." (Gen 22:6 8 NKJV).

There comes a time when you must trust God with your most important thing in life. Abraham dressed an altar to put his son upon, and in obedience to what he believed God would have him do, bound the object of his affection with rope. See this next portion with your mind's eye. With the stones and wood in place, Abraham very gently lifts Isaac into his arms, and places him there on the altar. In painful surrender to God, Abraham raises the sharp point of his knife over Isaac and prepares to slay him. With muscles twitching, and sweat beading on his brow, he faithfully places the life of his son in God's hands. But wait! As he prepares to release the "trigger," and plunge the tool of death into his son's throat, there is a stir in the thicket. A voice rings out from heaven, and as we read from the Bible:

"...the Angel of the Lord called to him from heaven and said, "Abraham, Abraham!" So he said, "Here I am." And He said, "Do not lay your hand on the lad, or do anything to him; for now I know that you fear God, since you have not withheld your son, your only son, from Me." Then Abraham lifted his eyes and looked, and there behind him was a ram caught in a thicket by its horns. So Abraham went and took the ram, and offered it up for a burnt offering instead of his son." (Gen 22:11–13 NKJV).

The New Testament provides us a commentary on what transpired there that day: "By faith Abraham, when he was tested, offered up Isaac, and he who had received the promises offered up his only begotten son, of whom it was said, 'In Isaac your seed shall be called,' concluding that God was able to raise him up, even from the dead, from which he also received him in a figurative sense." (Heb 11:17 19 NKJV). In other words, Abraham believed that if he did take his son's life, that God would restore it back to him again.

The parallel to Christ in this story is obvious. We have Isaac, forced to carry the wood for his sacrifice, just as Jesus was forced to carry His own cross to Calvary. Likewise Isaac trusted his father as he voluntarily was led to sacrifice, just as Jesus trusted His Father as He voluntarily gave His own life to be sacrificed. Isaac was the only begotten son of his father, just as Jesus was the only begotten Son. Finally, Isaac was figuratively raised from the dead just as Jesus was literally raised from the dead.

The reason I point out the parallels is to suggest that God understands and pioneered the pain of sacrifice and surrender. Who better to be able to empty life's tragedies upon? We may not see immediate healing, or have immediate reparation, or receive immediate attention. But I believe that in the end there is a place that brings catharsis and sense to life. It is a place of ultimate healing, where the godly ones receive their dead back from the grave, a place of no suffering, disease, heartache, or sadness.

It is a place my father often dreamed about as he laid suffering from the pains of angina. It is a place he reminded his children of, planting in them a quest to search after it. Jesus said: "… It is done! I am the Alpha and the Omega, the Beginning and the End. I will give of the fountain of the water of life freely to him who thirsts." (Rev 21:6 NKJV). I am grateful that my father led me to thirst after God, for I have not a spring of life within myself.

I think I know what it means to have God as my source of life. It has led me to an undeniable "touch" of His favor. I have had my roots driven deeply into the streams of His Spirit. When one has God as their source of life they cannot help but bear fruit, and, in times of draught they have no worry or fear, for God is there. As Jeremiah said:

> "…blessed is the man who trusts in the Lord, whose confidence is in him. He will be like a tree planted by the water that sends out its roots by the stream. It does not fear when heat comes; its leaves are always green. It has no worries in a year of drought and never fails to bear fruit." (Jer 17:7 8 NIV).

Jesus said simply one word to a frightened, desperate Peter on the water: "Come!" That is the word echoed down through the ages whenever men or women are broken, withered, and dying. When they are challenged to see more than the frail world they have grown accustomed to. When they are willing to step out of the boat of the ordinary, and experience the miraculous. Or, they long to know a source of life beyond themselves and their own "doings."

Maybe you can relate to Abraham or Peter, who in desperation needed a "brush" with the supernatural. "Come." It is a word through my father's posthumous example that I am still reminded of. It is a word I grew up knowing when I was hurting. And, it is a word I leave the reader with responsibility to choose in his or her own pain: "Come." "And the Spirit and the bride say, "Come." And let the one who hears say, "Come." And let the one who is thirsty come; let the one who wishes take the water of life without cost." (Rev 22:17 NASB).

"Morality is Relative"

Small Group Discussion Questions
Chapter Six Review

1. Have you ever witnessed someone's healing or deliverance, in ways spiritual, mental or physical, and wondered if God would ever do it for you personally?

2. When others observe your life do they see a "tree planted by the water?" Why or Why not?

3. Have you ever considered yourself the master of your fate or captain of your soul?

4. How does hope in God breathe life into otherwise bad situations? Define Biblical hope. [cf. Rom. 8.24–25 and Heb. 11.1]

5. Has God ever tested your level of commitment by asking you to give up something very special to you? How did you handle that?

6. Have you ever received the love of your "life" back after releasing it to God? Explain.

Chapter 7

Becoming Spiritually Defined

Your morality will be guided by what is defining your life. What you say, how you respond, your reaction to tragedy, what you do when you're cheated, all of life is guided by what is defining you. Furthermore, when life is defined by nothing, there is nothing to give moral accountability to. I think that destroys an individual in every aspect of life, because they are ethically unstable: "The integrity of the upright guides them, but the unfaithful are destroyed by their duplicity." (Prov 11:3 NIV). I also think it leads to the destruction of a culture: When there is moral rot within a nation, its government topples easily. But with wise and knowledgeable leaders, there is stability. (Prov 28:2 NLT).

In my mind, the lack of moral accountability has been the biggest contributor to our problems in education, business, and religion. We need to be reminded of a certain truth: "As we know Jesus better, his divine power gives us everything we need for living a godly life. He has called us to receive his own glory and goodness! {4} And by that same mighty power, he has given us all of his rich and wonderful promises. He has promised that you will escape the decadence all around you caused by evil desires and that you will share in his divine nature. {5} So make every effort to apply the benefits of these promises to your life. Then your faith will produce a life of moral excellence. A life of moral excellence leads to knowing God better. (2 Pet 1:3–5 NLT) When you know God better, the better you become spiritually defined.

I have heard that eagles go through an almost cruel ritual with their young. It really starts even before they are hatched. Mother eagle has meticulously worked on making a beautiful nest high up in the rocky crags. She has gathered such things as fur and feathers to ensure the smoothness of the nests inner lining. It is nothing but the best for her soon to be offspring.

Soon, her eggs are hatched and the young develop and mature into eaglets. With swelled chests, they test the wind that courses over their elegant home by flapping their wings excitedly into it. This is likely a sign to mother eagle, for she then does a rather extraordinary and baffling activity. Mother eagle begins to dismantle the beautiful nest she built. The hard work she put into making the nest is now used to abruptly tear it apart.

Bit by bit the smooth lining of the hatchling's refuge is taken out. Her objective is to make it as uncomfortable as possible for her developing young! Eventually, she jostles the little eaglet out of its sanctuary, forcing it to plummet towards the ground below.

With wings waving frantically, the little one gets its first taste of being out of the nest. The eaglet tries to fly, almost getting it from time to time, but gravity steadily plunges it towards the hard surface hundreds of feet below. Before disaster strikes, mother eagle races beneath her careening offspring, and scoops the young one up on the pinions of her wings, and deposits it into the safety of the torn up nest. Over and over again the lesson is repeated, until the eaglet finally flies on its own. As it soars now majestically above the earth, it is defined as an eagle, and sure of who it is.

That's exactly the image God uses to describe His relationship with us: "Like an eagle that stirs up its nest, That hovers over its young, He spread His wings and caught them, He carried them on His pinions." (Deu 32:11 NASB). Because God loves you, He will stir your nest!

There comes a time in our spiritual lives that we must learn to fly on our own, where we no longer depend on the "soft lining" of someone else's spirituality. There comes a time when we are forced out of our comfort, passing from the shadows of the beliefs of those who have taught us, into the light of our own revelation of truth. We must define our own faith, and choose for ourselves from the choices that lie before us in life.

At the age of fifteen, my spiritual "nest" was stirred, and I began to pass out of the shadow of my father's faith, into my own. It was then that my heavenly Father scooped me up on the pinions of His wings, over and over, until I learned to fly.

The Bible begins with these words: "In the beginning God created the heavens and the earth. Now the earth was formless and empty, darkness was over the surface of the deep, and the Spirit of God was hovering over the waters. And God said, "Let there be light," and there was light. God saw that the light was good, and he separated the light from the darkness." (Gen 1:1 4 NIV) Those words indicate the beginning of creation and life on earth. For me, they also represent the beginnings of my spiritual life.

"In the beginning God."

Being born and raised in the Christian church, God has always been a part of my life. The truth is, God is always at the beginnings of life, stirring in the heart of every human creature. The struggle against God is not due to a question of His existence, but the condition of our hearts. Non-truths build up there, establishing barriers of resistance towards God's love and mercy. Some of those non-truths leave us thinking that our spiritual definition is not important, that it is not so much what you believe, but that you believe in something, implying that all roads eventually lead to the same place. That is wrong thinking for this reason; when you believe in a speculative "everything," then you believe in a definitive nothing. Left with nothing, you will never find who you are spiritually.

As for me, I chose the wrong avenues to find who I really was. At the age of 15, I was slowly turning my back on my moral values. I was a recalcitrant young man, unmanageable by any authority figure in my life. I was hiding a pain that I was unable to release. I was desperately lonely, craving for acceptance, respect, and love. Being perceived as different was brutally hard for me. I couldn't understand how so very few understood that I had no control over being poor.

There is an enigmatic conspiracy when it comes to the poor. People perceive the poor as dirty, cursed, and unwilling to do anything to change their condition. It's uncomfortable to be around them, and so the poor exist in this conspiracy of silent suffering! Wrong treatment by others made me angry and vulnerable to spills of wrong behavior. I was drowning in a sea of self-pity and delusion. It wasn't long that I was labeled by teachers and family as a very "troubled" young man.

On one lonely occasion I was staring at myself in the mirror, feeling confused, guilty, and condemned. The tears that were streaming down my cheeks were releasing the poison that had been stored in my heart by believing the lie about who I really was. I was flushing out the anguish of old memories, all too painful to keep stored inside. I managed to make eye contact with the sufferer in the mirror, and swore fervently under my breath that day to live with a passion, either for or against God. Willing to give God first chance at my empty soul, I wept before Him in that moment, saying with a challenge: "God, do you love me? If so, then prove it to me!"

I had been taught about God's love all my life, but now, spiraling out of control like the young eaglet that was on a downward collision course, I was unable to believe that the God of love could possibly love a ruined, wicked life like mine. When I was painfully nudged out from my father's spiritual "nest," I flailed in the many "wind currents" offered by the world. God was soon to pick me up on His pinions, and carry me to greater heights, His heights, to the true spiritual winds.

Inwardly, I longed for the same strength that carried my father through the many hopeless years he lived in the shack. "In the beginning," God was at the heart of my spiritual life, creating in me a longing for Him, preparing to construct a new person out of nothingness, just as He had done in creating the heavens and the earth.

"Darkness was over the surface of the deep"

"The man without the Spirit does not accept the things that come from the Spirit of God, for they are foolishness to him, and he cannot understand them, because they are spiritually discerned." (1 Cor 2:14 NIV) Something cloaks the heart of a person who is in rebellion to God.

In the months following my oath to the "face" in the mirror, I was in and out of minor scrapes with trouble. It was after one such night of wasteful vexation, being drunk and feeling desperate, that I met my father at the door. The sadness written into my father's eyes cut me deeper than I know how to describe in writing. That moment has been etched into my memory. I cannot pry it free; it remains as God's reminder to me of where I've been. How difficult it must have been for him to watch the "Master Surgeon" carve away at the infection in the life of one who bore his name and carried his genes.

The hatred and disgust I was slinging out into society had taken its toll. I had become a beast, driven towards destruction and self centeredness. I blamed my economically poor background, I blamed the people that taunted me into feeling different, and I blamed the authorities in my life for not understanding my unusual reactions to situations that pushed buttons in me. I longed for someone to feel my hurt and loneliness. Darkness was indeed "over the surface" of my soul.

"The Spirit of God was hovering over the waters"

The word water in the Bible has commonly been known to represent God's Spirit. For example, John said in his book of revelation: "The Spirit and the bride say, "Come!" And let him who hears say, "Come!" Whoever is thirsty, let him come; and whoever wishes, let him take the free gift of the water of life." (Rev 22:17 NIV) And again, in Isaiah: "Come, all you who are thirsty, come to the waters; and you who have no money, come, buy and eat! Come, buy wine and milk without money and without cost." (Isa 55:1 NIV). Centuries before my father was born, God had made a promise to him as a man of God: "For I will pour water on the thirsty land, and streams on the dry ground; I will pour out my Spirit on your offspring, and my blessing on your descendants." (Isa 44:3 NIV).

The night I met my father at the door was the beginning of a series of events in my life that have defined me as a person. He "encouraged" me to leave my surroundings in Connecticut, and live for a short period of time with my sister in Georgia. Her husband was the pastor of a small church there, and my father felt the spiritual influence on my life would be cathartic to my damaged soul.

That time spent with my sister's husband formed a relationship between us that has been deeply rooted through the years following. He was my "kinsmen redeemer" of sorts, the "go-el" coming to my rescue, willing to pay the price to salvage me, to bring me into his home and share his very life with me. I got to hear him preach on Sunday, and watch his character on Monday. I respected and admired what I saw, human in his failings, but strong in his faith, a spiritually defined man like my father.

And so it was that somehow during my spiritual convalescence, between attending church, painting church facilities, and laughing with my "kinsman redeemer" over the squirrel we killed and couldn't eat because it looked too much like a little man, God began to soften my heart, and lift the cloud of darkness that was hovering over the surface of my soul. I was on the road to becoming spiritually defined. That was the summer of 1964, the decade marked by free love. God was about to show me what free love really is.

Much had transpired since I made my oath in the mirror, but I hadn't forgotten my challenge to God, I was having some deep thought about my spiritual future. I fell asleep in my sister's spare bedroom. During the night, God gave me a dream that troubled my spirit and sent me searching for answers.

I was standing inside a building when I heard a very loud commotion outside. Racing out of the building I looked toward the heavens and realized the source. I saw some figures in the sky, gradually descending, but I couldn't identify what, or who, they were. As they continued to descend I mentally pieced together the Scriptures that referred to Jesus' return. I then realized that they were angels, and, that the commotion I heard came from the blast of trumpets they were playing. The loudness was uncomfortable, piercing my ears with its shrillness.

I noticed a different figure in the middle of the angels that stood out above the rest. This figure was dressed in a long flowing white robe, hands outstretched toward the earth, as if inviting someone to come. I remember looking into His face. He had a look that I have never seen captured in a painting, nor does it bear description. It was a look of compassion, yet, it was resolute and holy. At the same time, I both feared and loved the presence of this figure.

By now, the ground around me had swelled with a sea of people, gathering to view what was happening. There were people of every age, gender, and race. Somehow it seemed we were all on equal level there, whether rich or poor, wise or simple, healthy or unwell. Indeed, I realized, this was the return of Jesus!

Fathers and mothers were holding their babies up to Him, other people just reached out their arms, calling out in joy: "Jesus, take me home with You!" And then, some just bowed on their knees in reverence. They all seemed to be so happy, but I was scared!

Then, God gave me a picture of two people groups, those waiting faithfully for His return, and those who were unprepared. The unprepared tore at their clothes with "wailing and gnashing of teeth." (cf. Mt 13.49–50) With a view that has been impossible to explain to others, God gave me an examination of myself that evening. I was not looking through a glass, I saw as though out of my body, and, I saw myself among the unprepared!

Having ripped at my clothes and flesh in agony, I then held up my hands to wave off His coming, and begged Him through my bitter tears: "Lord Jesus, please go back! Please don't come now! Do not end life yet."

I awakened from that dream, relieved that I was still there, but taking one very important step towards my spiritual awakening. I realized that deep within I really wanted to live with Jesus forever. The following day proved to be a day of reflection for me, and I asked my brother-in-law many questions. I pondered and queried over what had happened nonstop, consumed by that dream. I didn't sleep to well that following night, and by daybreak the questions of the previous day had not subsided. God's Spirit was at work in me, hovering over the surface of my own spirit, preparing me for what was about to happen shortly. Just as He had promised, He was pouring out "…water on the thirsty land, and streams on the dry ground …" (Isa 44:3 NIV).

"God said, 'Let there be light,' and there was light"

There's a Bible passage that reads: "the people living in darkness have seen a great light; on those living in the land of the shadow of death a light has dawned." (Mat 4:16 NIV) That is what literally happened in my life!

God had gotten my attention, and by the second night after that dream a great deal of thought had been processed concerning it. Once more, I had fallen into a deep sleep. It was a dark summer night in Georgia, and after several hours I was still sleeping, comfortably clothed in the warmth of my room. But something was going to be different about that evening, God had not forgotten about my challenge to Him.

I was abruptly awakened by the "fingers" of God stirring in the room. A glowing light had appeared at the foot of my bed.

Terrified, I sat up and pushed heavily back against the headboard of the bed, trying to back away, but I was pinned against the wall. When a man knows he is in the presence of God, his sinfulness becomes utterly sinful.

The light was somewhat mesmerizing, and I fixed my eyes upon it. I gazed into its brilliance as it grew brighter and brighter, like waves of the ocean coming ashore, increasing in strength with every passing wave. It flooded the room, and I peered around a bit to see if I could locate where I placed personal items, testing to see if I were really awake. I was fully awake that evening! I could see every item in that room, as the light was so brilliant it shone as though it was midday.

I realized that the brilliance was centered at the foot of my bed, and turned back to it. It was then I understood the source of light. God had not sent just any light; He sent the light of His cross! There it glowed, resplendent in glory, inches from where I lay. The cross I saw was an empty cross, Jesus is no longer there. He has accomplished the mission, the purpose set before Him, the release of sins captives. And, I was one!

That night, God communicated this thought into my spirit: "I love you!" They were just three simple words from a powerful God who showed me an empty cross, a cross where Jesus had once died for me. As an answer to my challenge, God had brought the cross to where I was; lonely, self pitying, devoid of love, and desperately in need of a Savior.

The glory of the cross I saw that night slowly faded away and was engulfed in the darkness of the room, but the glory of the cross where Jesus died never fades. It forever remains the focal point for release and blessing, or, for bondage and curse. Every form of sin was brought to death there on behalf of those who ask for help, but also, every act of God's judgment is passed there on behalf of those who refuse to ask. The choice determines the outcome!

We all face the "stirring of the nest," we all come to a point of making a solo flight, and choosing for ourselves what we will do about Jesus. "Let there be light" is the pleading of God for all men. "For God so loved the world that he gave his one and only Son, that whoever believes in him shall not perish but have eternal life." (John 3:16 NIV)

"He separated the light from the darkness"

I have never understood why God answered my challenge. For that matter, I guess I've never understood how God's incredible love could possibly extend to me. I am humbled by that fact after nearly forty years of serving Him. In those years, God has not always chosen to answer my "challenges" in such a powerful way. I think on the whole, God is pleased with those who trust without test. It is from Job we gain appreciation: "Though He slay me, yet will I trust Him …" (Job 13:15 NKJV)

For whatever God's reason, I'll never forget that summer of 1964. For that year in a tiny spare bedroom, located in the back of a modest parsonage, which was built for a little church, at a small town deep in the heart of the South, far from my home in Connecticut, were those two events that God chose to "separate the light from the darkness" in me. They were a stirring of my nest, and the launching of my own spiritual definition. I began to soar as an eagle on the currents of God's truth, knowing I would be carried on the pinions of His wings before plummeting to my death. I was enjoying my new discovery of who I was as I glided across the skies of His Word. Little by little He stripped away the pain from the years of sorrow I had as a child. I began to see, and care about, who I was from God's perspective. It truly matters what we are defined by!

My wife and I have dedicated our lives to His service, and to the great cause of proclaiming His love to others. It is for that cause that I teach and write, and it is for that cause that He has made me. I stand therefore, to point out a slowly decaying truth; that we are not defined by what we have, but by what has us.

When God sets His mark on a man, He draws that man to Himself, separates the darkness from the light, and declares that man as His. What that man has, the world cannot duplicate or take away, for that man knows who is his, and whose he is. When a man knows that, he has become spiritually defined.

"Morality is Relative"

Small Group Discussion Questions
Chapter Seven Review

1. Has God ever "stirred your nest?" Were you able to fly, or did He return you to the nest?

2. Do you think everyone goes through a time of spiritual rebellion?

3. If you were brought up in church, was there a time when you knew that you needed to make your own choices concerning spiritual matters?

4. Was there ever a time in your life when the "lights" just seemed to go on for you? Why do you think that happened?

5. Have you ever broken someone's heart by something you said or did? How did it feel?

6. Would you say that you are spiritually defined?

Section #3

The Third Lie: Life Has No Value

Preface to Lie #3

There are now over six billion people living on this planet.[19] With the advance of modern medicine, people are living to ripe old ages with fairly good quality of life. However, in spite of this, the value of life has decreased of late. We are told by "authorities" who ought to know better, that we are mere accidents. On the other hand, the idea of teaching intelligent design is frowned upon in the learning institutions, the preference being to tell people that man has evolved from the waters. The story goes that somehow through a freak accident of cosmic activity there was a charge of electrical voltage into this body of water that started microscopic life forms into existence. The "soup" ingredients, it is suggested, were in just the right conditions for life to start. And now, after billions of years of evolution, man is what he is today.

I can't think of anything more disheartening than to think that I came to earth as an accident, will have no real purpose for my existence, and then perish without hope of ever having life again. It's no wonder that people can so easily abort a baby, or take on a "live for today" attitude. The truth is, it is a lie. As David said to Saul: "As surely as I valued your life today, so may the LORD value my life …" (1 Sam 26:24 NIV). My hope in the next few chapters is to remind you that God does value your life.

Metamorphosis

I have a friend that I met during my college days. My first impression was that she was emotionally fragile. She walked around campus holding her head down, never making eye contact or speaking. She was withdrawn, and I felt extremely sorry for her. It seemed that she and I could have written the same stories concerning our self-abasement. I wondered how she had gotten that way, what was hiding under the cover of the quick smile as we passed each other? In my mind I had scrapped her as socially incorrigible, a disheartening result of something gone foul within her convivial structure. I saw no hope of recovery from that.

I had lost contact with most of my college classmates after graduation, and, was therefore surprised to see her at a function we were both attending some fifteen years later. Even more surprising was the way she handled herself. She was talkative and pleasant, a true joy to be around. A remarkable transformation had taken place in her life. Later that evening I learned that she was to be the keynote speaker. I listened as she sang and spoke, holding on to every word she said, being amazed at the miracle I was witnessing before my eyes.

I couldn't wait to pose the obvious question of what had

changed in her life. Here is her story told to me that night: after graduation, she had settled into a good job with a decent company. She rapidly rose through the ranks, reaching as high as she could go in the firm. Her personal life seemed to be going just as well. She had a wonderful church family, and was using her talents there. She was happily involved in the music ministry, and was working with the teens.

Earning a decent income with an excellent company, and having a healthy church commitment, she appeared to have successfully merged her spiritual and social life. But, she knew that something was wrong on the inside. She was feeling discouraged and sad; a victim to the lie of worthlessness, and it was lying dormant in her psyche, damaging her emotions as it reared its head from time to time to convince her of her inadequacies both physically and spiritually.

One night after returning home, burdened with an empty feeling of sadness and despair, she fell on her knees before God and wept bitterly. Through the sobs she uttered this reminder to God concerning a Bible passage she had grown familiar with: "God you promised me 'abundant life,' but, my life is empty and dissatisfying! Why don't I have abundant life?"

As she contemplated those words, she felt impressed to look them up again. To her amazement this is what she read: "The thief comes only to steal, and kill, and destroy; I came that they might have life, and might have it abundantly" (John 10:10 NASB). Most people, like she had, forget the first part of that verse. There is a truth in that passage that God wanted her to get that night; Jesus did come to bring us abundant life, but, there is a lying thief in our midst, an "accuser of the brethren," a morbid killer of our souls.

The liar had done his best to rob her of worthiness and value. Now, armed with God's truth, she rose from her knees with a new determination to accept who she was in God's sight. She flatly rejected the lies she had grown to embrace over the years. It was that result that I had been listening to as she delivered the evening's keynote address.

Many Christians never seem to get it, and live their lives in constant self condemnation, clamoring for self worth outside of the realm of God. The following is God's recipe for recovery. It is found in the writings of Paul, to the Church of Rome: "And do not be conformed to this world, but be transformed by the renewing of your mind, that you may prove what is that good and acceptable and perfect will of God" (Rom 12:2 NKJV). In my study of that verse, I've discovered three crucial Greek words that Paul used.

Word # 1—Conformed
"Do not be conformed to this world."

The Greek word translated as conformed is *suschematizo*. *Suschematizo* is made up of the following two words: *"Sun,"* indicating a resemblance, and *"Schema,"* indicating something that has been fashioned.[20] *Suschematizo* therefore means to fashion something that has a resemblance of something else. That's where the English word schematic comes from.

A schematic is essentially a blueprint. It is an electronic diagram for a component, in order for technicians to do their repairs. Wires or circuits make little sense in the back of a television without a schematic, or blueprint, to label and indicate them.

Paul advises, do not be a schematic of the world. That is, do not believe what the world says you look like. The world will always give a distorted image of who you are. Remember passing by those funny mirrors at the carnival? They were intended to be distorted images of the real you. They either made you look tall and skinny, or short and fat. Imagine if you lived in a house where you had only those kinds of mirrors. If you never went out, these would be the only images that you could use to base how you looked. You would always envision yourself as either tall and skinny, or short and fat, and, you would believe that others saw you that way too.

The image that was embraced by my friend, and I, was based on what the world had told us about our lives. It was not a physical distortion, but rather a mental and spiritual distortion. Conforming to the world's schematic is embracing the world's definition of worthiness. It is allowing your mind to be patterned after that which the world says you look like. But remember, that is a distorted view. The world may say that nobody really loves you, but God says: "I love you." (cf. John 3:16 or John 13:34). The world will say you are not able, but God says: "You can do all things through Christ." (cf. Philippians 4:13). Maybe you have guilt, but God says: "I forgive you." (cf. I John 1:9 or Romans 8:1).

The world's image of life and God's image of life are at odds, and have been since the entrance of the liar to the Garden of Eden. Yet, some Christians still choose to live by that insane ungodly image, desperately trying to fit into the world's 'schematic." Paul says "do not be conformed," because that is a lie!

Word #2—Transformed
"But be transformed"

The word transformed is the Greek word *"metamorphoo,"* and it means to be changed or transfigured.[21] It is from this word that we get the English metamorphosis. Before becoming a butterfly, a caterpillar goes through a stage known as "chrysalis."[22] The fragile chrysalis process changes the fuzzy caterpillar into an awesome butterfly with wings of elaborate designs and powerful colors. The metamorphosis process is total in that the creature is completely changed. Even the internal organs look differently.[23] In the end, the completed creation has transitioned from crawling to flying. What a transformation we see, as the butterfly spreads its wings to the breeze and flies off in majestic fashion. The end result is much different and more beautiful than how it began.

The caterpillar's chrysalis process symbolizes how Jesus can transform you into something beyond your imagination and hopes. Spiritual chrysalis is growing beyond yourself, opening your life to Jesus' power and love. In our word study, Paul is saying that God gives us opportunity to be changed from our ugly, "worm-like" emotional and spiritual state, to a profoundly new and beautiful creature. My friend was transformed in just that way, and in no-less spectacular fashion than the metamorphosis of a caterpillar.

So, concerning our mental or spiritual state, we can, and should, emerge from the world's "cocoon" embrace. We are not to believe the distorted blueprint images that the liar has held before us, rather, we are to be changed into something God says about us. How does that happen?

Word #3—Renewing
"By the renewing of your mind"

The word renewing in the Greek is *"anakainosis,"* and it means to restore something to its original design.[24] The concept is that of restoring an antique car. Those that do so painstakingly attempt to make their antique as original as possible by using either original or closely replicated parts. God desires that our minds be restored as closely to the original as possible, that we may see ourselves as God originally intended, free at last from the serpents lie.

When I surrendered my life to God, I experienced that. It was a night and day difference for me. In fact, it felt as though an immediate release had occurred, as though the demonic forces that had been pressing upon my emotions were suddenly sprung from their moorings. Prior to Jesus becoming a part of my life, I had considered myself a lesser human being, misfit and unattractive.

I guess that's the point really, Jesus changes lives! He is the source of renewal that we need, we cannot do it alone. Our part is to respond by faith, that is, to embrace with deep conviction the truth God has given. When I accepted and believed God's opinion of me, I discovered I was "…fearfully and wonderfully made …" (Psa 139:14).

Again, there are two mirrors for our souls to look at; we either see the world's image with its distorted carnival mirror, or, God's reflection of ourselves through His Word. Though God does not force your choice about these options, there is a pleading man inside all of us to be rescued from the lie that keeps us scrambling in the world for acceptance, success, and love. There is a place in the realm of God where you can be restored in your mind, where you can agree with God's assessment of your value, and be loosened from the thief's influence "that you may prove what is that good and acceptable and perfect will of God." (Rom 12: 2 NKJV).

> Where broken vows in fragments lie
> The toll of wasted years,
> Do Thou make whole again, we cry,
> And give a song for tears.
> Transformed by grace Divine
> The glory shall be Thine[25]

"Life Has No Value"

Small Group Discussion Questions
Chapter Eight Review

1. How does "the world" dictate to you what you look like or even what you are?

2. How can we avoid the world's definitions of acceptance and love?

3. Have you ever experienced an instantaneous change in outlook about yourself?

4. In what ways has the thief tried to steal from you?

5. In the process of spiritual restoration, what percentage of the "original" are you? What area of restoration do you still need help in?

6. Have people ever told you that they see a change in your life? Is that important?

God Heals The Desperate

Everybody has been desperate at one time or another. My friend, brother, and I had just come up from the swimming hole, a muddy old farm pond located along a winding dirt road that led out to a cow pasture near where I lived. After checking for bloodsuckers, we decided to take a short cut back home. Hanging onto our loose clothes, we squeezed through a barbed wire fence and picked up the pace across the field.

Several cows had been watching us from a distance, and, to be sure, we were keeping our eyes on them too. Swiftly and without warning, one of the larger animals broke from the herd and started to charge. She had a huge set of horns and was rumbling rapidly toward us.

My friend knew the cows, as they belonged to his dad, the owner of the small farm. He had encountered this mean one before. He was trying to get the big cow into a milking stall, but she wasn't cooperating. Even though he shouted and pushed, the cow showed no signs of moving. In desperation, my friend picked up a long two-by-four that someone had leaned against the barn wall. He really wasn't sure what he would do with it, but figured to use it as some sort of reinforcement to his command. Also, it provided a bit of protection, "just in case." My friend and the cow fixed their gaze on one another. The cow apparently wasn't intimidated by the two-by-four and charged at him.

With eyes widened in fright, my friend screamed out at the top of his lungs, let loose of the two-by-four, and darted quickly out of the barn. The old mean cow had barely gotten into her charge when the loose two-by-four came crashing down, hitting her solidly on the head, and sending her bellowing into the milk stall!

It was that same old mean cow that was now lumbering after us, as we walked exposed in the open field. "Head for the tree," someone shouted, and we sprinted toward a lone Oak tree. I tossed aside the loose clothing I was carrying under my arm, freeing myself from the extra load, and ran as fast and hard as I could.

My older brother and friend quickly made the tree, jumped for a limb, and had climbed up safely out of the cow's reach. Because I was younger, and couldn't run as fast, I was much slower reaching the tree. What seemed like an eternity passed, and I finally reached the tree, totally exhausted. But, because of my size, I couldn't find a limb to climb up on. Frantically I jumped, grabbed for anything, tried to shimmy, whatever it took to reach safety. I knew if I could just reach the hands of my big brother, that I would be safe. I trusted my brother. My brother was strong and was always there for me.

I was charged with fear and could barely think straight when I heard my brother's firm voice directing me to give him attention. "Listen to me," he said "Reach up! Reach up as high as you can and I'll grab hold of you." I turned around long enough to see that the mean cow had lowered her horns into place and was rapidly closing the gap between us. I reached my hands in blind confidence towards my brother, stretching as far as I could, leaving myself in a vulnerable position to the charging cow. In relief

I finally felt his strong grasp. Just like in the movies, he valiantly lifted me to safety just as the large animal reached the base of the tree where I had just been standing. I looked down from the safety of my perch in the tree, sizing up the huge animal that snorted below, realizing how close I came to being seriously gored.

Spiritual desperation is just like that. We stand at the base of life's tree, frantically screaming for help. Jumping and struggling to make it, we cannot reach the safety of the limbs on our own. The lie says to walk away. With a deistic or fatalistic slant, the lie says either God does not hear or does not care about your cries for help. But walk away with the enemy lowering his horns at you? That's spiritual suicide. But that is what so many do, turn away from the only source of help in their time of trouble.

What will it take for you to cry before God? What will it take for you to reach up to the limbs of heaven? It may be that He's waiting for your point of desperation. Spiritual desperation is a step towards healing. I believe you will never go after a full measure of God's healing for you, unless you become sick and tired of the self-condemnation, guilt, or despair that you are living with. You must become desperate for God's help. You must become desperate for His love to hold and embrace you closely.

I know I've just raised a few eyebrows, but a man's nature will not lead him to repentance, and therefore healing, any more than a man's laziness will lead him to work, unless he's starved! The truth is that a man's nature is "lazy" toward repentance because of sin. Even the "star" of the New Testament said: "I do not understand what I do. For what I want to do I do not do, but what I hate I do. {16} And if I do what I do not want to do, I agree that the law is good. {17} As it is, it is no longer I myself who do it, but it is sin living in me. {18} I know that nothing good lives in me, that is, in my sinful nature. For I have the desire to do what is good, but I cannot carry it out." (Rom 7:15–18 NIV). Paul constantly felt desperate before God, calling himself the "chief" or "worst" of sinners." (cf. 1 Tim 1:15).

The prophet Jonah was on the run from God. For three days and nights he lived inside a great fish. I can't imagine what it would be like to live inside the bowels of a huge fish. I wonder if he was overwhelmed by the smell of digesting flesh, or getting weaker and weaker because he had so little oxygen. What I do know, is that this dark, lonely, and desperate place is where his prayer originated from, for it is said of him: "From inside the fish Jonah prayed to the LORD his God.' When my life was ebbing away, I remembered you, LORD, and my prayer rose to you…'" (Jonah 2:1+7 NIV).

There are so many folks who have been swallowed up by a great "fish" called consumerism, moral agnosticism, or a valueless, worthless life. That is desperation! That is reaching the point of spiritual and emotional exhaustion! That is when we must fall to our knees sobbing those words that can change life forever: "God where are you? Where is my abundant life?" From the belly of the vacuous world system that has swallowed them up, they must, in their desperation, remember the Lord.

How do you personally remember God? Jonah no doubt remembered Him as the God he was running from. Many remember God as an angry stepfather, waiting for them to fail, waiting to punish them for every wrong. Many remember God as the daddy that moved out when they were so desperate for his love. Many remember God as the insensitive Supreme Being who allowed a certain tragedy to occur.

Our perspective on God, or how we remember Him, often

determines how we approach Him, either out of love or out of fear. But, the two seemed to have blended with Jonah didn't they? After his ordeal Jonah said to God: "…'O LORD, is this not what I said when I was still at home? That is why I was so quick to flee to Tarshish. I knew that you are a gracious and compassionate God, slow to anger and abounding in love, a God who relents from sending calamity.'" (Jonah 4:2 NIV). On the other hand, in deep respect of God's power he fearfully prayed: "…You hurled me into the deep, into the very heart of the seas, and the currents swirled about me; all your waves and breakers swept over me. {4} I said, 'I have been banished from your sight …'" (Jonah 2:3+4 NIV).

God loves His creation, and perceiving that encourages us to live a consecrated life. However, the fear of God is an important element in our spiritual lives as well. After three months of trekking in the wilderness, Israel had reached the base of a mountain in Sinai. It was not just any mountain, it was the "mountain of God," it was the place God spoke audibly to Moses when the Ten Commandments were passed to the nation. God had Moses summon the nation to the foot of the mountain, but warned them to keep their distance, punishable by death for whoever dared touch it. Three days later the mighty power of God erupted out of heaven with thunder and lightening. A thick cloud veiled the mountain, as if to separate the holiness of God from the profane lives of the people. The "voice" of God cracked through the distant fume of fog in the form of a very loud trumpet blast, sending the people into a trembling frenzy. The people begged Moses not to let God speak to them for fear they would die. Moses response is enlightening: "Moses said to the people, "Do not be afraid. God has come to test you, so that the fear of God will be with you to keep you from sinning." (Exo 20:20 NIV).

Did you get that? The fear of God is our weapon against sinning! God knew the hearts of those people wandering in the wilderness, and He knows our hearts too. How easy to fall victim to the lies of the "wilderness" we live. How easy to lust after the things we left back in "Egypt" from which we came. Respect, through fear, for the One who can snuff my breath out with a shout, initiates my approach to Him, as I am reminded that this "wilderness" in which I live: "...will be destroyed by fire, and the earth and everything in it will be laid bare." (2 Pet 3:10 NIV).

But again, our relationship with God cannot be driven by fear alone. The Bible shows that we have a sympathetic God who is willing to step lovingly onto the pages of life. It is by understanding that love that we are encouraged in our faithfulness and obedience to Him. That was illustrated to me by the actions of a cat named *Chicle* (pronounced Cheeclay).

The cat belonged to my son who had moved in with us for a short stay while he was waiting to move out of state. *Chicle* was young and curious, constantly trying to escape outside either by ripping apart screen windows with his claws (we once caught him by his rear legs suspended halfway through the torn out screen) or diving out the door behind unsuspecting folks as they left the house.

With limited success making it outside, he turned his attention to the novelties around the house. We rescued him once as he was hanging by two front paws off a doorway after sliding down a stairwell some twenty feet above. He found his way into dresser drawers, between sheets, and anywhere his inquisitive zest for life and action would take him.

My wife was preparing a lunch one morning before she left for work. Closing the refrigerator door behind her, she made her way over to the table to fix a sandwich. After a few minutes, she heard a sound coming out of the refrigerator. Opening the door again, she found beloved little *Chicle,* sitting on top of a leftover chicken carcass, gnawing away for all he was worth, oblivious to the potential danger of being left there all day.

My wife scooped him up, still clutching his catch, and a bit angry to be disturbed. Cute as it was, we knew if this behavior continued, it could potentially harm him. We all got together later that night discussing how you can discipline a kitten. Someone suggested we try filling a spray bottle with water and gently deter *Chicle* with a squirt when he was doing something that could harm him, or that was just distasteful for him to do, such as, eating the butter out of the butter dish left out, or walking through the sugar bowl.

Loading our bottle, we set it aside specifically for use on the furry little guy. Shortly, I was to have my first, and I might add eye-opening, opportunity to use "the bottle." I had walked into the kitchen and found *Chicle* on top of the table, working over the vestiges of breakfast that had not yet been put away. Finding the spray bottle, I sprayed it a few times and sent him flying off the table and through a doorway leading into an adjacent room.

Now that was pretty easy I thought to myself, but wondered where he charged off to. I looked for several unsuccessful minutes but couldn't find him. Mystified, I gave up and walked back into the kitchen, only to find *Chicle* sitting up on the table again, seemingly unmindful that I had returned, rather innocently enjoying his "feast." So again I sprayed him with the bottle, sending him scurrying off to the other room.

It proved to be an interesting lesson for me, for after several attempts a pattern had developed. The spray bottle came out and the cat disappeared. This went on for several hilarious minutes, leaving a memory that more soberly translated to my own relationship with God. I realized that the momentary obedience the little cat showed was based on his fear of the spray bottle. Regrettably, we couldn't communicate our intentions more clearly to him. We were concerned for his well being, not wanting him trapped in a refrigerator all day or escaping through a chewed out window screen into the busy road we lived next to.

As with *Chicle*, it is difficult to live in compliance with God if we live continually, or only, in fear of His "spray bottle." Eventually something seems to give and we end up running away before the "trigger" can be squeezed. Obedience apart from love is at best a strain. Realizing that, God extended His love first: "This is love: not that we loved God, but that he loved us and sent his Son as an atoning sacrifice for our sins." (1 John 4:10 NIV).

Chicle didn't realize our love for him, and, unfortunately, we could not communicate that to him. A cat is not programmed to communicate with a human in that way. But, God has programmed you in His image. He has given you a seat of emotions, and, He communicates to those areas by His Spirit and through His Word. That Word is given with us in mind and based on love for us much like the spray bottle was based on love for Chicle. In reciprocation of that love Jesus said: "If you love me, you will obey what I command." (John 14:15 NIV).

Understanding God's love for you is the basis for understanding His commands to you. Conversely, understanding your love for God is the basis for you following those commands. It is not only out of fear of the spray bottle that we obey God, but also out of love. And so that is the balance of love and fear. They are the essence of maintaining a proper perspective of God, and therefore, of living a life of Godliness: "Through love and faithfulness sin is atoned for; through the fear of the LORD a man avoids evil." (Prov 16:6 NIV).

Yet, because of the lie, many have had a disconnection in their relationship with God, leaving them feeling out of His favor, and, therefore, out of His love. Sadly, some folks are unwilling to let go of the lies, preferring to hold on to ethereal images of economic, occupational, and social success. It reminds me of a story I heard several years back. A little girl named Ruth had gone shopping with her mom. As they were checking out, Ruth spotted a pearl necklace. It was an imitation piece, rather inexpensive and cheap looking really, but it glowed with the brilliance of the faux pearls it was made with, catching the six-year-old's eye.

Ruth just had to have it, and begged her mom unmercifully. Her mom thoughtfully answered: "Ruth it's almost the time for your birthday, and you know grandma usually sends you some money at that time. And if you do some extra chores around the house, I'll pay you extra in your allowance. Save up your money, and you'll soon have enough to buy the necklace."

Ruth went home and worked very hard at doing some extra chores for her mom. Her birthday came, and sure enough, grandma sent some money along with a card. Patiently and diligently she worked and waited until she figured she had enough saved to buy the necklace she had set her heart on.

Returning to the store, Ruth rushed in excitement to the counter where she had seen the necklace. Scooping it into her hand she placed it next to the register and waited for the cashier to total it up. "Three dollars and seventy five cents" the clerk said. Ruthie reached into the little sack she had been saving her money in. Out she dumped the coins. Quarters, dimes, nickels, and pennies all scattered over the counter. The clerk tolerantly counted out the three dollars and seventy five cents worth of change. Ruthie had enough, and with a little left over to buy a piece of gum!

The clerk packed the items into a bag and handed them over to Ruthie, who pulled the necklace out and immediately put it around her neck. She wore the necklace everywhere she went, from school to the playground, and whatever the circumstances, even refusing to take it off when taking a bath or going to bed.

One night Ruthie was sitting on her dad's lap, listening to a bedtime story. Dad finished, closed the book, and then looked his little girl in the eyes. "Sweetie," he asked, "Would you give me your necklace?" Little Ruth was horrified and quickly responded, "Oh daddy, you know I love you very much, I would give you anything, but please don't ask me to give you my necklace! You can have my bike, or the baby doll I just got for my birthday, only please don't ask for my necklace."

"It's okay sweetie," her daddy said. He put her into bed, tucked her under the covers, bent over her and as he bent down, he brushed her cheek with a kiss saying: "I love you very much." "I love you too daddy." Ruthie responded, and they hugged, both saying "goodnight."

A few days passed and Ruthie's daddy was finishing up with another bedtime story. Again she was sitting on his lap, feeling half asleep, laying her head into his chest when he asked: "Sweetie, are you ready to give me your necklace?" Ruthie responded with the same anguish as before, and meekly threw her arms around her daddy saying: "O daddy, if you only knew how much I love my new necklace. I will give you anything else that I have, anything at all, but please, don't make me give you my necklace."

"Don't worry sweetie," her daddy said with a trace of tears in his eyes, "I would never make you give up your new necklace if you really don't want to." With that he placed her in bed, cuddled her in his arms for a moment, brushed her cheek with his own unshaven one, and gently kissed her goodnight.

A few more nights and bedtime stories passed by. Once more Ruthie was sitting in her daddy's lap, feeling his warmth against her cheek that was lying on his chest. Only this time Ruthie was silently crying. Her little tears had soaked daddy's shirt, but he was unaware of what was happening inside his baby girl.

Holding out her hand to her daddy, she opened her palm to reveal her prized possession. It had never come off since she had left the store weeks before. Now in a flood of emotion she held it out in sacrificial surrender to her father saying: "O daddy, I love you more than anything I have, even more than this new necklace. I want you to have it now." Fighting the tears now gathering in his own eyes, her daddy slowly took his baby girl's "offering" out of her quivering tiny hand. "Thank you sweetie," he said, and then reached into his pocket, pulling out a blue velvet case with a strand of genuine pearls, a stunning necklace, an exquisite family heirloom passed down from his mother. He softly placed it around her neck, somehow envisioning her all grown up. How beautiful she looked, he thought, how deserving an heir. "Sweetie," he said in a whisper, "I've had this waiting for you this whole time, I was just waiting for you to give up the one you so cherished."[26]

Isn't that a picture of God? He wants to give us His best, the real thing in place of our artificial dreams. He offers us so much more than the lie of what we cherish, yet we are often unwilling to let go of it. We live in a culture where life has been given little value. God has been given a back seat to various other avenues of acceptance, love, and discovery of who we are. It is my conviction that some will never come to "remember the Lord," until they stand at the base of the "tree," or lay in the belly of their own "great fish." No, some will never come to "remember the Lord," until they finally come to Him with utmost desperation, tired of the lies in their lives, tired of reaching for the limbs that are just slightly out of reach. Only then will they reach up in blind faith to a loving Strength, waiting above to pull them up to higher ground, to the limbs they cannot reach on their own.

"Life Has No Value"

Small Group Discussion Questions
Chapter Nine Review

1. Why does God heal the desperate? What is it about desperation that points us toward God?

2. Have you ever reached a spiritual tree that you were unable to climb up in? Discuss? How, if at all, did you finally get up?

3. Do you think that everyone needs at some point in their life a big "brother" to help them get up the tree?

4. Discuss the statement that "the fear of God is our weapon against sin."

5. In the story of Ruth and her necklace, how are we like Ruth? (Give examples from your life).

6. Has there ever been a time when you held tightly to the "lie" only to find out later that God had something better for you?

Chapter 10

Big Rocks

I was driving south on Interstate 95 through Connecticut, just having had lunch with one of my parishioners. I was pretty much in a hurry, as it seemed all on the roads were that day. Work was waiting for me, and I had several miles to go to get there. As I came up upon a car that had veered off the road, I noticed that several older ladies were waving white handkerchiefs, trying frantically to signal someone over from the rushing traffic. Those were the days before cell phones, and so, the ladies' efforts were at the mercy of their little white cloths.

Everyone was speeding past them, and, I too was trucking right on by, when their desperate looks caught my attention. Finally slowing my car, I eased onto the shoulder of the interstate. Putting the car in reverse, I backed up to the stranded women. They were all huddled in a group around the driver's side door. It was then that I noticed the slumped over body in the seat. Apparently, having felt the beginnings of a heart attack, the driver managed to get the car out of traffic and stop it on the shoulder of the thruway before sliding into unconsciousness. Her efforts saved the lives of her passengers.

We finally managed to get the attention of an EMT, but, despite his best attempts, the woman died on the way to the medical center. The experience was surreal and all too graphic, only reinforcing the Biblical adage concerning the frailty of our lives: "As for man, his days are like grass, he flourishes like a flower of the field; the wind blows over it and it is gone, and its place remembers it no more." (Psa 103:15 16 NIV).

Experiences like those remind us of the important things in life. Unfortunately, it is those important things in life that seem to get such little time from us. Such things become less prioritized as we fall into the lie that says we have more valuable things to get done right now.

I heard about this college professor who was teaching his class about time management. He took out a vase and placed three large rocks into it. He then held it up before his class and asked, "Can this vase hold any more?" All agreed it could, so the professor added some much smaller stones to the vase, which trickled their way around the big rocks, and, worked their way to the bottom. The vase was looking pretty full, so the professor asked again, "Can this vase hold any more?" Hesitantly, most of the class agreed that it could, so the professor added some sand into the vase which worked its way into any tiny gaps between the big rocks and the smaller stones already in place. The vase looked absolutely packed as the professor held it once more before his class, "Can the vase now hold any more?" he asked. Almost no one thought it could, so the professor reached under his desk and pulled out a pitcher of water he had hidden there. He proceeded to pour the water into the vase until it saturated rocks, stones, and sand, leveling off at the brim with absolutely no space for anything else. "What does this illustration teach you about life?" he asked his class. Immediately hands shot up from everywhere. He pointed out one young lady sitting towards the front, and she answered with what the entire class was undoubtedly thinking, "If you work hard enough at it," she explained, "you can always find the room for one more thing to put into your vase." "No," the patient professor replied, "the real lesson is this: if you want to get the big rocks in, you had better put them in first."[27]

My father seemed to understand that concept. He took the time for the "big rocks" in his life. To see softball games, get ice cream, take rides in the car, and to make family memories at holidays. As his children, we knew that we were of utmost value to him.

Furthermore, I admired my father's intense devotion to the church, and his personal commitment to Bible study and prayer. The lie we have been told to value, deadens the need for the values of my father. It is almost more honorable to work on Sunday, than to bring your family to church, and we are getting too busy to dedicate much time to personal spiritual life.

The lie says if we give our family the valuables, such as a roof over the head and a certain amount of pleasant things, then our struggles have been worth it, and that we have given enough. The truth is that there are still certain "big rocks" that our families need.

Convenience! We live in a convenient society. It was not convenient for drivers to stop for the older ladies waving a white handkerchief on the side of the interstate. It is likewise not convenient to get up Sunday morning after a tough week, and bring your family to church. Convenience plays a part in spending one on one time with a child, spouse, or needy friend.

The Bible says Jesus was regularly inconvenienced. With His popularity, He probably could have called the people to where He was. He probably could have held a citywide crusade in downtown Jerusalem or Nazareth. I imagine that would have drawn great numbers of people, and, it would have been very convenient for Jesus. But if He had done that, what would have become of the Samaritan women at the well, or the Gerasene demoniac, or the leprous men outside the city. They were social outcasts; one considered morally "loose" with many "husbands," one was a raving lunatic who the city kept in chains, and the others no one would touch out of fear of contamination. It is unlikely that they would have been at, or invited to, a crusade in downtown Jerusalem. But, Jesus refused to let convenience, prejudice, or public opinion interfere with the important things in His life. He went to where they were, and left each of them with an encounter that changed their life forever.

Under the Father's direction, He walked through the "Samaria's" of this world, talked with the riffraff of the land, and gave equal opportunity to all. By putting others before Himself, He set the pace for those who are following after Him. They are the husbands learning to practice self-sacrifice toward their wives, the parents toward their children, neighbors toward one other, and mentors toward their followers. The main message of the Gospel tells the story over and over, love is not convenient, and when people allow their lives to become convenient, they become loveless.

The beautiful stream that we see flowing down the mountain's side during spring is made crooked by following the course of the least resistance. Beautiful people are like that too; they are made crooked by following the convenient course of life! We need to take a good look at our hearts. Are we becoming what we do not want to be because of the structure of our environment?

In 1991, "Promise Keepers" began to address the issues of

male absenteeism in America, particularly in the areas of family and spiritual matters. Based on its popularity, it seems to have struck a chord. In 1970, James Dobson authored "Dare To Discipline," a book on parenting, that was instrumental in rearing my own children. He is now head of "Focus on the Family," an organization committed to Biblical family principles. The call of these organizations, and many others, is for us to take time to put the "big rocks" back into our lives, and reassess the values of our spiritual forefathers that we have so steadily strayed from.

The atheist's son was at his side, visiting him on his deathbed. The son had been taught well by his father, and he too was now an atheist, fully embracing a Godless belief system. In those moments before his father's passing, the son saw how deeply he battled against dying. As the father called out in agony and fear, his son pleaded to him with these words: "Father, just hang on." The father grasped his son's hand in his, and with one last dying breath uttered these final words to his bewildered son: "Son, hang on to what?" That is the question I pose to this society. What are we hanging on to? Why does it take holding a dying person in our arms to remind us that the big rocks in our life must be put first? Or a letter from our wife's attorney to let us know we've spent too much time away? Why did we miss our child's game, or just time to snuggle?

People are not so much remembered for great things accomplished. I can't tell you who the five wealthiest people in America are, and, as much as I love sports, I cannot remember who won the last five Superbowls, or NCAA Tournaments, or Heisman trophies. Nor do I remember who the Oscar winners are from this current year, or the last few Nobel Peace Prize winners. Do you? Most people probably don't.

No, the people who pass through your life will not remember you for the great things you accomplished, but for how you touched them personally. It's the personal touch that shows what you value, what you consider "big rocks." While I may not remember the winner of the last Nobel Peace Prize, you know who I do remember? I remember Mrs. Flowers. She was my fifth grade teacher, and her students had value to her, she considered us "big rocks" in her life.

There was a girl in our class that year whose face was severely scarred when her clothes were set on fire, melting her flesh and nearly taking her life. Apparently, she had gotten too close to a stove. The fire not only left her disfigured physically, but also left its mental scars. She was often all alone, with no one who would befriend or talk to her. Some, despite her involuntary mutilation, taunted her for her ugliness. She was different, and all in our class avoided her. I am ashamed to say, even me. I of all people should have known better. I knew what it was like to be taunted and friendless because of something I had no choice in.

One day, Mrs. Flowers had heard enough. She knew what was taking place at recess and in the hallways. At an opportune time, when the little disfigured girl was out of the room, she addressed us together as a class. It was for her speech that day that I have remembered her for over 40 years. With scolding boldness she verbally portrayed what it would be like to be that little girl who had no friends. It was a picture I had not previously considered, an image I did not want to embrace, an emotion hitting too close to home. What was it like to be her? I pondered over and over again on what Mrs. Flowers had said. How often did she go home feeling friendless and desperate for someone to understand her? How often did she cry herself to sleep? I understood quite well what Mrs. Flowers was saying!

God used her reprimand to massage compassion into the calloused composition of my twelve-year-old heart. It was shortly thereafter that I met Barbara at a convenience store down the street from where I lived. She and I were there for the same reason. Each of us hoped to buy a candy bar with the small amount of change we held in our hands. She was before me at the checkout counter, and after looking over the rack of candy, chose one that cost just a bit more than she had. The store owner told her she needed to make another selection. I saw the disappointment on her face, her heart was set on that candy bar, and for just a couple of pennies she was unable to get it.

In that moment, God tested me. Mrs. Flower's speech was still ringing in my ears, and I knew that girl needed a friend. I reached into my pocket and took out the few pennies she needed to get her candy bar and placed them into her hand. Nothing could have prepared me for that little girl's response. Our eyes locked on one another, she with that ugly face that had been scarred by a nasty fire, and I with scarring in a place no one else could see. We communicated with each other that day through a way hard to describe. She gave me thanks for something she considered that I had done that far transcended the few coins I placed into her hand. She thanked me as friend to friend!

Her words of appreciation were for the willingness I showed to touch her with sympathy instead of apathy, and for an act of kindness instead of cruelty. It was a moment that stirred my soul to the core. I was humbled beyond measure, and walked from that store as a twelve year old boy who had learned a spiritual lesson that some adults have yet to learn. Jesus came to touch the things the world considers ugly. He touched me in my ugliness. Some people will never get it, even as they said about Jesus back then, they still say today: "…Why does he eat with tax collectors and 'sinners'?" (Mark 2:16 NIV).

The Nobel Peace Prize is awarded to a person who has worked towards maintaining peace, dignity and human rights. They care about those who others think are a burden, and those too ugly to touch. In spite of their fine efforts, I remember very few of those people, but, Mrs. Flower's "Nobel Peace" speech to her fifth grade class has been a part of me for over forty-five years, and I have remembered the point. She worked towards human rights and dignity for the children in her care. She took the time to plea for her students to stop the abuse! Mrs. Flowers took the time to address the "big rocks" that we represented in her life.

I don't remember who won the latest Grammy Award, but I remember my mother gently singing, almost in a whisper, into my ear as a child. I was an active preschooler, so mom had me take a nap as a daily routine, probably to give her a break. I fought against naptime vehemently, for it interrupted my busy little schedule from all the activity filling my day. Mom, in her wisdom and love, would put aside her agenda to lie down for a few minutes next to me.

She would sing these incredible songs she learned from a pastor's wife when she was a child. They were in Swedish, so I never fully understood the words, but the melodies were sooth-ing, and her voice sweetly reflected her love to me. The sounds were cathartic, and, along with her warm embrace that cuddled me against her breathing chest, I listened for her heartbeat as I soon grew weary and fell asleep.

It was those waves of love that were wafted to me by her gentle voice that I looked forward to. They surrounded my spirit, bathing me in tenderness. As much as I fought against it, I inwardly sought after those precious moments of naptime with my mom, moments that have never been erased from my love banks for her.

She passed earlier this year at the age of eighty-three, and I am now fifty-six, but up until her death I would ask her to sing her Swedish songs when I saw her. Though she has never won a Grammy, her remarkable ability to sing into her active little boy's spirit deserved far more. She made me one of the "big rocks" in her life.

As remarkable as yesterday's Nobel or Grammy winners are, very few of us can remember them. These folks were considered the best in their fields, yet we generally cannot distinguish them for their performances. It is our mentors, our friendships, those who have spoken lasting words, and the ones who have made us feel appreciated or special that we remember. The people who have made a difference in your life aren't the ones with the most credentials, the most money, or the most awards, but the ones who valued you as one of their "big rocks." What will you do with your "big rocks?"

> "Not everything that can be counted counts,
> and not everything that counts can be counted."
> Albert Einstein[28]

"Life Has No Value"

1. How have Christians been too busy to do the things of God? Is the church paying the price for that today? Do people give to support churches or needs?

2. In what ways does our checkbook reveal our values?

3. Have you ever failed God because of inconvenience? Did it have an effect on your relationship? How did it get resolved, if it did?

4. Discuss the statement: "Why does it take holding a dying person in our arms to remind us that the big rocks in our life must be put first."

5. What are some of the "Big Rocks" you have taken out, only to realize now that the "Big Rocks" should be first?

6. Name someone who has impacted your life positively because they valued you as one of their "Big Rocks."

Section #4

The Fourth Lie: Males Are Meaningless

Preface To Lie #4

I enjoy football, and, this season, I enjoyed watching what I consider to be one of the better college running backs that I've seen in awhile. As he was giving his acceptance speech for having won the elite Heisman Trophy this year, his eyes brushed over the audience and landed on his stepfather. His voice, halting from time to time as he kept back the emotion, began to waver as he now fought back the tears that began to flow defiantly. Thanking the many important people in his life, Reggie Bush was now thanking his stepfather. He is the picture of what a "real man" is, he said, because he had taken Reggie into his life at the age of two, and raised him as his own. That struck me! An athlete, who was used to getting battered by 280 pound defensive linemen, defined true manhood with the example of a man who chose to raise and mentor him through love and relationship.

In a "Rolling Stone" obituary article about Harry Chapin, it read: "Harry Chapin often described himself as a "third-rate folk singer," and judging from most of the reviews he received in these pages and elsewhere, he wasn't only kidding. Yet Harry Chapin was something more than that. For many who knew him, he was a legitimate hero, not so much for his music as for his consistent and conscientious willingness to fight the right battles, to stand up for a just cause, no matter how hopeless."[29] There was one "just cause" in a song that Harry Chapin was specifically known for. In it, he wrote the stinging lyrics about the responsibility of fathers to their children. Here is a sampling:

> My child arrived just the other day
> Came to the world in the usual way
> But there were planes to catch and bills to pay
> He learned to walk while I was away
> He was talkin fore I knew it
> And as he grew he said,
> 'I'm gonna be like you, Dad,
> You know I'm gonna be like you.'[30]

These lyrics tend to tell a truth. Even though friends, the media, the culture and so much else will have an impact on the life of a child, the things that will be permanently etched in their lives will be the values and dreams of their parents. Fathers have a specific role in that. We live in a fractured society. It is not good for any society to have as many absentee fathers as we have today. The father figure is important. He brings something to the family union that God intended for only him to have. Men are different than women, and children need them both.

In an article on feminism from Wikipedia, it states that: "A large portion of feminists are especially concerned with what they perceive to be the social, political and economic inequality between the sexes which favours the male gender; some have argued that gendered and sexed identities, such as "man" and "woman", are socially constructed. Feminists disagree over the sources of inequality, how to attain equality, and the extent to which gender and gender-based identities should be questioned and critiqued."[31] And again from Wikipedia in an article on radical feminism: "Radical feminism believes that the root of the problem is patriarchy itself. Therefore, the radical feminist calls to dismantle the patriarchy altogether to solve the problem. The extreme radical feminists call for the destruction of the entire male sex, as shown in Valerie Solanas' misandrous writing, SCUM Manifesto."[32]

Many women have been severely damaged by an oppressive male culture, or by "fathers" who have raped them sexually and emotionally, or by the "glass ceiling" in place by the organizations that they work for. Nina Baym expressively writes: "Many of us had been severely damaged or at least painfully threatened by psychoanalytic pseudo-explanations that pathologized our intellectual aspirations as penis envy or masculinity complexes. Many of us had experienced the terrifying reality of father-figures whose need to seduce us far exceeded our desire to seduce them."[33] There are ongoing tragic stories of male domination that make me embarrassed to be called by that gender. But their actions are not what God envisioned for the man's "helpmeet," the very "bone of his bones." [cf. Gen 2.23]. In God's eyes, there is equality of gender, but a role for each: "There is neither Jew nor Greek, there is neither slave nor free man, there is neither male nor female; for you are all one in Christ Jesus." (Gal 3:28 NASB). "And God created man in His own image, in the image of God He created him; male and female He created them." (Gen 1:27 NASB).

I've expressed the former only to say that the next three chapters are not intended to be an "equal time" reprisal to woman's rights, but rather an admonition to men. It is a call for them to be what God intended for them to be, mentoring men who are gauged by the measure of God.

The Bridge Builder
By Will Allen Dromgoole

An old man, going a lone highway,
Came, at the evening, cold and gray,
To a chasm, vast, and deep, and wide,
Through which was flowing a sullen tide.

The old man crossed in the twilight dim;
The sullen stream had no fears for him;
But he turned, when safe on the other side,
And built a bridge to span the tide.

"Old man," said a fellow pilgrim, near,
"You are wasting strength with building here;
Your journey will end with the ending day;
You never again must pass this way;
You have crossed the chasm, deep and wide-
Why build you a bridge at the eventide?"

The builder lifted his old gray head:
"Good friend, in the path I have come," he said,
"There followeth after me today,
A youth, whose feet must pass this way.

This chasm, that has been naught to me,
To that fair-haired youth may a pitfall be.
He, too, must cross in the twilight dim;
Good friend, I am building the bridge for him."[34]

The Rogue Elephants

I recall hearing a story about several young bull elephants being raised on a protected reserve in South Africa. They were shipped there years ago as orphans when their parents were culled due to an over abundant population near a farming area. Not too long after they arrived, employees realized that an abnormal number of rhinoceroses in the same reserve were dying. At first, there was grave concern that poachers were doing the killing to harvest their horns, but, upon further investigation, they discovered that the orphaned male elephants were growing up to be bullies. They were attacking the smaller rhinoceroses! That was never heard of before, as elephants did not normally attack rhinoceros in their natural settings.

Realizing the problem was with the orphaned elephants, someone came up with the idea to bring several adult male elephants into the reserve. That mix of the adults with the younger male orphans surprisingly worked. The adult males took their places as the reigning rulers of the reserve, and kept the younger ones from bullying the rhinoceroses.

An interesting conclusion was drawn from the experiment. The game reserve experts said that the missing factor in the orphaned elephant's lives was that they never had male adults to correct behavior or "teach" them how to act properly toward the rhinoceroses.[35]

If that is true for the animal kingdom, how much truer it is for humanity. We need male mentors! When I grew up the television show "Leave It To Beaver" featured a close knit family with a strong father figure named Ward Cleaver. Ward was portrayed as a man of integrity and character. He had wisdom, patience, understanding, and a loving relationship with his sons and wife. Today, Ray Romano plays the role of husband and father in the sitcom "Everybody Loves Raymond," and portrays his character as a bumbling mess, insanely conniving his way through life. You get the impression he never can quite figure out his wife, true for many of us, and that he strains to come up with the proper counsel for his kids, as he blunders through one episode of life after another. Invariably, no one seems to pay much attention to his insights or thoughts. Though I find the show incredibly funny, it probably reflects the thinking of the day.

Just in my life span I have seen the complete reversal of the male role depicted on television. If it's true that television reflects the culture of its time, then our culture, in just one generation, has taken a reversal of the male role too. That leaves us facing a dearth of male character models. I've heard it said that in ten more years the male gender will not be necessary in the proliferation of humanity, and by implication, the family.

The lie in this case is that a normal vision for society can survive without a normal vision for family. My vision for family is a healthy male leadership figure and a healthy female co-partner in the general harmony of structuring healthy children. In keeping with the elephant orphan example, I believe that what we're seeing in our societies rogue teen behavior has a direct relationship to that leaning toward the attitude that men in a family structure are meaningless.

Recent stories from the County I live in are a few examples. One teen tried to kill another three times, but was unsuccessful. One girl slashed her victim with a knife, while her friends broke his jaw and knee caps. A nineteen-year-old argued at a store with a sixteen-year-old before shooting him to death. Figures from our County show that in 2004 seventeen persons between the ages of six and thirteen were charged with violent crimes, such as, rape, assault, and armed robbery. The following year, 2005, another seventeen youths were charged in violent crimes, with eight of them being between the ages of ten and thirteen.[36]

One of the worst beatings I ever witnessed was by a fifteen year-old boy against another. I was employed one summer as a work leader of disadvantaged teen boys. It was a program oriented towards kids from families of low income, those with one parent, or with some other physical or social handicap. One jobsite was located near a lake, so I promised to let them take a swim on their lunch break the following day.

They brought their trunks to work, we stopped for lunch, and the boys disappeared into a bathroom that they used to change their clothes. In what seemed to be a matter of seconds, one of the teens came running towards me, eyes wide with fright. Two of the boys had gotten into a pre-planned fight, and nobody was able to break it up.

I charged into the bathroom, slamming open the door, and faced a bloody scene. I thought that one of the boys must have been stabbed! I couldn't mentally embrace the thrashing I was seeing. The apparent victor in this battle was showing no signs of letting up. He held the other boys head by his hair, and leaning him over he was jerking it up with powerful force, then slamming his face back down into a knee being driven up brutally from below. Not once, nor twice, but repeatedly, on and on the beating continued as blood was hurled against the bathroom walls, and the loser was kneeling in his own fluid of life. I thought he might die on the spot! The entire group of us could not intervene in the relentless massacre. He was a madman! No screaming, no emotion, just an assassin doing his job.

I had a hard time getting my mind around the whole scene before me. How could a young man of fifteen show no signs of mercy, sorrow, or pity for his victim? How could this young man continue to bleed out the life of another with absolute stoic rage? And then I remembered. I knew something about that young man that very few knew. Just months before I got him on my work crew this young man repeatedly watched as his father callously punched and kicked his mother. One night, he listened to her screams, her begging for life, her plea to be left alone, and this young man reached for a knife, pulled his father away from his mother, and plunged the knife deeply into his father's heart, killing him on the spot.

Now I ask you, if the emotional "scabs" from this young man killing his father are still lingering over the wounds to his suffering spirit, if a young man still is haunted by the memories of that night, how do you pull him off of a victim who had been taunting him? After killing your father, what is it to fight against the world? Never mind another fifteen-year-old.

Our culture needs family, and a family needs a proper father. Both the father and the mother bring into the mix of child rearing the necessary male and female combinations to nurture the appropriate things into their children. A mother is generally responsive and protective, whereas a father encourages chance and adventure. My wife and I had different reactions to situations involving our children. For instance, if a child came running to us after tumbling off their bike, her reaction was an immediate embrace to her breast, undisturbed by the bloodied nose that was ruining her new blouse. My reaction was instinctively different. I analyzed the situation to find out the extent of injury. If it wasn't serious, I would think of getting him off the rug that he was bleeding onto. My wife's intuitive response was what our children needed, but so was mine. She brought them sensitivity, while I figured bloodied noses just came with riding bikes.

Most men cheer their children to "go for it," even joining in to make that leap across a racing stream. Most wives yell out their customary "be careful." That is the way God made husbands and wives, instinctively different, and children need that balance in their lives.

Fatherhood doesn't come easily or naturally for most men. Instead, they tend to "see it" by those whom they are fathered by. Just like the orphaned bull elephants, the young men in our culture, who are themselves often "orphaned," need an example to observe. By seeing the "fences" that mark misbehavior, where the lines are drawn, and the gentle touch of people that care, they can bring into their own families the necessary fatherhood attributes needed to nurture their own sons and daughters.

We're seeing a passion rising from the hearts of today's youth. It's both good and challenging. They want relevant truth, and they want it expressed in both word and deed. They no longer will stand for the "do what I say" dialogue, they long to see integrity. Too many troubled youth are brought home by the "knap of the neck" after a night of wild adventure, to be met by a father propped up in an easy chair. "How many times have I told you to stop doing that," dad says, while he sips on his "adult beverage" and puffs on his "fix." Don't miss the point, I'm not judging what's right or wrong for you, I'm judging what is more important, the right to do a certain thing, or the message it may speak to someone you love. Today's youth are challenging us; "what is the difference between what you tell me, and what you do?"

Integrity is an interesting word, having its roots in the word integer. I can remember using the word integer back in a modern math class in Jr. High School. We learned then that an integer was a whole number with no fractions. The word integrity represents a wholeness that is entire and undiminished, as in, soundness of moral principle and character.[37]

It is safe to say that a person of integrity has moral fiber and respects God. There are no fractions of truth in that person. He is absolutely whole in his honesty and dealings with others. The Bible says: "The righteous man walks in his integrity: his children are blessed after him." (Prov 20: 7 NKJV). I can tell you this; I am blessed because my father walked in integrity, and I have diligently pressed to give that to my children.

With few exceptions, I never had to check myself around my children. There were never "adult" times or situations that my children could not be a part of. I didn't watch television programs when my kids were in bed, that I wouldn't watch if they were sitting next to me. I didn't choose to say or do things away from my family that I would not say or do in their presence. That pattern kept me from moments of slipping up around them. I know my life, I know my tendency to do wrong, and I know my family is one way that God chooses to constrain me. For me, that "glass house" exposure to my family was, and is, a welcome restraint of sin.

My sin, and failings, as a husband and father were before them, and, they often heard my pleading for their forgiveness. I was not too proud to let them hear my broken repentance before God. As a father and mentor, I lived before my family as a man naked and ashamed of my sin, but also, as a living example to them that the mercy and forgiveness of God is long reaching.

The point is, doing right comes from the heart. The morally sound man or women does not have to concentrate on it. It is the fruit of one's character, the outflow of their life. It is not contrived, turned on and off, or only done in certain situations. Jesus said: "A good man out of the good treasure of his heart brings forth good things, and an evil man out of the evil treasure brings forth evil things." (Mat 12:35 NKJV).

Moral mentoring is a lifestyle of action and words, of example and raw heart exposure to those being led. It is allowing those you are mentoring to see the real you, your sin and failings, but also, your surrender and brokenness before God. Our cultural problem with rogue males is not due to lack of discipline alone, but a lack of moral mentoring. You cannot beat moral truth into anyone, but you can live your life a moral example before them, that they are brought to a place of considering your example when choosing for themselves from the many "ethical" pathways of life.

I applaud the spiritual hunger seen in many of our youth, and the demand they make to see integrity by their leaders. What saddens me is that so often they have come to the table ready to lay down their lives and follow, only to be disappointed by those they look upon who have nothing of moral value to offer.

Where have all the moral mentors gone? They have been weakened and compromised by the impurities within. That is where weakness finds its root, from within, working against the heart with influences that shouldn't be there. I'll never forget the time my father took me to work with him at the foundry. I was eight years old, and had never seen the sights and sounds of the foundry before. I watched anxiously as they melted the metal in the furnace, poured it into the large caldrons designed to hold the molten mixture, and finally as they poured it into the molds they had prepared.

As the metal was poured it looked like a lava flow, reddish orange in color, rather tempting to reach out and touch. But as it cooled an ugly scum formed, like a scab, over the top. I watched as they scraped it off carefully, before pouring it into the molds. In bewilderment I asked my father: "Dad, what is that crusty stuff on top, and why do you scrape it off?" "That's called dross," he said, "it's all the dirt and bad elements the metal had in it before we heated it, and, if you don't get it out, it weakens the piece that you're making."

I've thought back over that many times through the years, because, I find there is spiritual dross in my life. It surfaces under extreme pressure, by the "fires" of temptation, and gathers there to cover the surface of my heart, waiting for me to either scrape the scum off, or to have it weaken the vessel of my life, the "piece" God is trying to make.

There are many mentors who are compromised by the dross impurities, because, they have never scraped the scum that forms on the surface of their hearts. In time, that leads to shallow opinions, and open-minded answers to moral questions. But morality is never gray. God asked one of the greatest leaders and mentors in Israel, King Solomon, what he would like to have. He answered: "… give your servant a discerning heart to govern your people and to distinguish between right and wrong …" (1 Ki 3:9 NIV).

Absolute right and wrong are what the children of our culture need and want, truthful answers, and practical ways to apply that truth to their lives, through the loving application of a man's example and leadership. Instead, they are often seeing hypocrisy. They get the giving of counsel, but not the living of counsel. Men are becoming marred by the impure dross surrounding their heart. In God's mercy, it is coming to the surface of their hearts time and again when the heat is on, but they aren't taking opportunity to scrape away the scum while the metal is still workable.

The Bible says that David was a man after God's own heart [Acts 13.22], but, when the fires of temptation came through a bathing Bathsheba, the dross of sin covered that heart like scum. One horrible evening: "... David got up from his bed and walked around on the roof of the palace. From the roof he saw a woman bathing. The woman was very beautiful, and David sent someone to find out about her. The man said, 'Isn't this Bathsheba, the daughter of Eliam and the wife of Uriah the Hittite?' Then David sent messengers to get her. She came to him, and he slept with her ..." (2 Sam 11:2-4 NIV).

David could have become a casualty, but God sent Nathan, a man of moral integrity to scrape the scum away (cf. 2 Sam 12:1-9). When David saw his heart, and that he was not the leader God would have him to be, this is what he wrote in repentance: "Create in me a pure heart, O God, and renew a steadfast spirit within me. {11} Do not cast me from your presence or take your Holy Spirit from me. {12} Restore to me the joy of your salvation and grant me a willing spirit, to sustain me. {13} Then I will teach transgressors your ways, and sinners will turn back to you. (Psa 51:10–13 NIV).

We need a resurgence of men who are moral leaders. We need men who are willing to have their hearts torn in repentance, and who turn to God for the hard moral answers. My father set an example before me that I never saw "strained" out by the colanders of life. Never was he "not home" when the uncomfortable phone call was for him. Never did I see him cheat an individual or bring home "samples" from work. He spoke decently to my mother, trusted in his children, lived by his word, and was respected in the church and community. He was a man who feared God, a man of prayer who borrowed from the sources of God's wisdom and discernment.

He was not a perfect father, but, I remember his longsuffering and patience. I enjoyed sitting next to him in church, for he had a certain way of rubbing the back of my neck, tenderly putting my restlessness to ease. It seemed at just the right moment he would reach into his pocket, pulling from it a licorice flavored candy which kept me satisfied for some time. A half of a century has passed since those days, but they are so melded into my memory that I remember them being far closer in years. They are a fond emotion of nostalgia. My father was firm, yet tender. As his son, I feared his discipline, but cherished his touch of love.

There are many young rogue males in our culture who will become casualties unless God sends a mentoring Nathan into their lives, a man of integrity who will never lose the fear and shame of doing wrong, nor fail to stand up boldly for truth.

"Success without honor is an unseasoned dish;
it will satisfy your hunger, but it won't taste good."[38]

"Males Are Meaningless"

Small Group Discussion Questions
Chapter Eleven Review

1. Does the depiction of God as Heavenly Father bring you an emotion of joy or pain? Why?

2. Do you think the media conveys the general trend of the culture? Explain.

3. Have you ever experienced hypocrisy? Was it from someone in authority? How did it make you feel?

4. In what way has the "dross" in your life risen to the surface?

5. How do you define a white lie? How about integrity?

6. In what ways have you been a mentor?

Will You Take This Woman?

A young man stands waiting in the front of the church. He is sharply dressed in his tuxedo, best man to his side, waiting anxiously for his beautiful bride to march down the isle. Soon she arrives, her veil concealing the sparkle of joy and excitement on her face. Her father lifts the veil to kiss her cheek, and then places her hand in the hand of the groom in a symbolic gesture saying: "I trust you to take care of my daughter as I have taken care of her." Vows are read, and promises are made in the presence of God and the witnesses who have gathered.

Finally, the preacher turns the couple towards the congregation, and, announcing an amazing miracle that the "two have become one," states that they are husband and wife. Hand in hand they leave the church as a married couple, but do they really know that they are just at the beginning of a path to discovering what that relationship is all about?

I still think back and laugh about it from time to time. I was discussing relationships in the car with my son. My wife was riding in the back seat and listening carefully to my "words of wisdom." I had told my son that "love" between his mother and I had developed through the years, and that I had desired to marry her because she was a "nice person."

I noticed the change in her demeanor almost right away. She was not so talkative, and seemed to have a lot on her mind. The next morning we dressed for church with relatively few words. I didn't think much of it because my wife isn't a morning person, but, the ride home from church wasn't much better. Even a few tears managed to surface and roll down her cheeks.

I was concerned about what was going on, so I sternly ventured something to the effect of: "You need to tell me what's happening!" She responded with a biting tone and quivering voice: "It's all your fault!" "What's my fault?" I asked in surprise. "You said you married me because I was a nice person," she replied. My only response was, "But you are a nice person, what's wrong with that?" She continued, "you didn't say you married me because you loved me, you just thought I was a nice person."

Needless to say, I spent the next hour or so trying to explain my wording. I still don't know if she fully understands what I was trying to say, but, she did manage to get some relief listening to "Focus on the Family's" broadcast the next morning. The speaker seemed to be saying the same things I had been trying to communicate to my son.

Male and female relationships are sometimes difficult. My wife and I had been married for over thirty years when the former incident occurred. Communication is not automatic, and neither is our understanding the role of husband or wife. To the man, the Bible advises: "Husbands, love your wives, just as Christ also loved the church and gave Himself for her, that He might sanctify and cleanse her with the washing of water by the word, that He might present her to Himself a glorious church, not having spot or wrinkle or any such thing, but that she should be holy and without blemish. So husbands ought to love their own wives as their own bodies; he who loves his wife loves himself." (Eph 5:25 28 NKJV).

That's an interesting admonition. The husband is to love his wife as "Christ also loved the church." Christ selflessly gave Himself to the church, all of Himself, on Calvary. He has set the church apart for Himself, and has acted upon her in such a way that she would become a "glorious church."

The word "glory," *doxa* in the Greek, is understood as brightness or brilliance.[39] When describing something it can be thought of as "shining forth," or reflecting that item. That is, the glorious church shines forth, or reflects, who Christ is, in the sense of His character, His attitude, and His personality. The point of that Scripture is one of comparison. As Christ has selflessly loved, pruned, and cared for the church she has become His reflection, or Glory. Likewise, as a husband selflessly loves, prunes, and cares for his wife, she too will become his reflection. That is, she too will be selfless, loving, and caring toward him. Referring back to the previous scripture, a husband striving to live out obedience to God's Word before his wife finds he is presenting to himself a glorious reflection of himself through his wife. Put simply, what a man sows into his wife he will reap again. If you spend enough time listening to and watching a man's wife and family, you will eventually learn much about the man himself.

To the wife, Peter says: "Your beauty should not come from outward adornment, such as braided hair and the wearing of gold jewelry and fine clothes. {4} Instead, it should be that of your inner self, the unfading beauty of a gentle and quiet spirit, which is of great worth in God's sight. {5} For this is the way the holy women of the past who put their hope in God used to make themselves beautiful. They were submissive to their own husbands …" (1 Pet 3:3–5 NIV).

So why is it so hard for a man to love his wife as Christ loved the church or for a woman to be "submissive" to her husband as the Biblical Sarah was? Just as God intended union, Satan has intended separation! Just as God intended that the "two will become one flesh," so Satan has authored the writ of divorce!

Since the fall of man, Satan has intruded on God's best. The fall not only introduced man to physical death, but spiritual death as well: "… they heard the sound of the LORD God walking in the garden in the cool of the day, and the man and his wife hid themselves from the presence of the LORD God among the trees of the garden. Then the LORD God called to the man, and said to him, 'Where are you?'" (Gen 3:8,9 NASB). God, in His omniscience, obviously knew where Adam was physically, but questioned Adam as to his spiritual whereabouts. That is, the condition of his heart and the reason for his "hiding."

The torn spiritual condition between mankind and God carried over into every aspect of Adam and Eve's life, including their relationship with one another. As a result of the fall, God informed the couple that the following curse had entered into their relationship. Speaking to the woman, God said: "… Your *desire* will be for your husband, and he will *rule* over you." (Gen 3:16 NIV–Italics Mine).

I believe that verse holds the key to understanding marital breakdown. It answers the question of why "men are from Mars" and "women are from Venus," that is, why it is so difficult for male and female to have a union of view. There is a curse on the marriage relationship! Just as the fall has brought curse on every other aspect of human affairs, it too has brought disaster into the marriage. God intended that: "... the two will become one flesh'? {6} So they are no longer two, but one. Therefore what God has joined together, let man not separate." (Mat 19:5–6 NIV). That is precisely what Satan has torn apart in the fall. Take a good look at the curse.

While women will battle the urge to be unyoked from their husbands, men will react to that with unbearable control, or "rule." Both are wrong! After the curse, Eve's "desire" would be "for her husband." I don't think the curse involves a physical desire only, which probably wouldn't be such a curse, but that she will desire the role of her husband. At the same time, Adam's response is to "rule" his wife. Again, I don't take that to mean a normal relationship of leading, but an "iron fisted" control of the wife, far from the example of Christ as "head" over the church He loves.

The words "desire" and "rule" are used again in the chapter following the description of the curse. Here Cain, the brother of Abel, was upset with God because: "... Cain brought an offering of the fruit of the ground to the LORD. Abel also brought of the firstborn of his flock and of their fat. And the LORD respected Abel and his offering, but He did not respect Cain and his offering. And Cain was very angry, and his countenance fell. So the LORD said to Cain, 'Why are you angry? And why has your countenance fallen? If you do well, will you not be accepted? And if you do not do well, sin lies at the door. And its *desire* is for you, but you should *rule* over it.'" (Gen 4:3 7 NKJV—Italics Mine)

The Aramaic words *teshuwqah* {desire} and *mashal* {rule} are used in both passages of Scripture. According to Strong's Concordance, *teshuwqah* has the sense of "stretching out after" something.[40] And, the Hebrew *mashal* is best described as dominion or rule by power.[41] Applying that sense to the passage of Scripture concerning Cain's battle, sin was "stretching out after" him, but he must exercise a "powerful rule" over the temptation happening in his spirit.

Remember that God's admonition to Adam and Eve was based in response to their fallen state. For the woman to desire her husband doesn't seem like much of a curse, but for the woman to be consistently in contention with his role as husband is. Likewise, for a man to lead his wife is not a curse, but for a man to have an unhealthy rule over his wife is. The curse says wives will struggle in their wills to be "submissive," and that husbands will "rule" over them. God's way is for wives to be like Jesus is in His "submission" to the Father, and for husbands to be as Jesus is in His willingness to lead the church in sacrificial love.

If you apply that to the curse on marriage, an interesting concept emerges. Neither partner understands or desires to stay in the roles God intended. Who wants to be in a position of submission to another person? Or, who wants to be responsible for making final critical decisions for others? But, that is precisely what God intends for the institution that He has chosen in which to raise Godly offspring?

The word "submission" causes many women to recoil with emotion. To some it means resignation and conformity, a losing of one's self-identity and equality. Rest assured that God sees no difference in gender when relating to Him. She is to have: "…honor as a fellow heir of the grace of life …" (cf. 1 Pet 3:7 NASB). The Biblical use of the word "submission" means to voluntarily come under someone. It is the word *hupotasso* in the Greek, which is made up of the words "*hupo,*" meaning to place under,[42] and "*tasso,*" which means to have a sense of devotion to.[43] It is an act of placing one's self under the realm of another that is respected. It is used when Peter says for young men to "submit to your elders" (cf. 1 Pet 5:5), or when Paul suggests that some have not "submitted to the righteousness of God" (cf. Rom 10:3). The idea of *hupotasso,* or submission, is to give oneself to.

Like most other things in life, submission is a choice, and is done voluntarily, as "unto the Lord." [cf. Eph 5.22]. It is to understand God's place for your life as wife and mother. Though according to the Garden of Eden curse, it may be difficult at times to lay down your life for the sake of order and union, keep in mind that Jesus willingly submitted Himself to the will and order of the Father, and went to Calvary to offer there His very blood.

Jesus gladly found Himself as the second person in the Trinity. That was not as a matter of position or equality, but of order and role: "Jesus answered: "Don't you know me, Philip, even after I have been among you such a long time? Anyone who has seen me has seen the Father. How can you say, 'Show us the Father'?" (John 14:9 NIV). That was His position, and yet we read: "Father, if it is Your will, take this cup away from Me; nevertheless not My will, but Yours, be done." (Luke 22:42 NKJV). That was His role as Messiah. In the same way, families need women who will be like Jesus, taking their roles willingly before Him.

God knew the special place that wives would hold for their husbands. He looked around after creating Adam and said: "…It is not good for the man to be alone. I will make a helper suitable for him." (Gen 2:18 NIV). It is in the midst of a wife being a "helper" to her mate that the marvel of Biblical submission comes into play. It is the mystery of how she can so meekly and selflessly give of herself to another. The essence of it is captured by Bette Midler in a beautiful song she wrote about a friend. It is how I feel towards my "helper."

"So I was the one with all the glory,
while you were the one with all the strain.
A beautiful face without a name for so long.
A beautiful smile to hide the pain.
Did you ever know that you're my hero,
and everything I would like to be?
I can fly higher than an eagle,
for you are the wind beneath my wings."[44]

I was wandering around the funeral home with the manuscript of my mother's memorial service in hand. I was feeling worn out from the sadness. I knew what was in it, and wondered if it would comfort or create emotional chaos for my siblings. I also wondered if I could get through it personally.

Many were gathered into small circles, remembering my mother with respect and silent applause. Some memories were to be cherished, while others were still too painful to be pondered upon for very long. There was some laughter, and lots of polite conversation going on. In the midst of that, I suddenly felt all alone.

I hunted for my wife, asking several if they had seen her. Finally, someone pointed her out, and I went to seek refuge from my best friend. As I drew near I whispered into her ear that I was in need of prayer. She pointed to a secluded place in the large room, placed her hand in mine, and together, hand in hand, we left the clamor behind to get alone for a moment with our Lord.

Praying softly into my ear, she led us before Him who is able to heal the broken-hearted and mend wounded soldiers. I parted with her, spiritually refurbished for the moment, and prepared to deliver a sensitive eulogy of my mother. Her love helped soothe the raging sadness within. Her love helped ease the barrage of fiery darts being hurled at my emotions, her love eased the pain.

I share that only to make a point. It was one of many acts of love from my "helper" that helped me hurdle that difficult moment. She has willingly placed herself under my life as wife, living out what I believe to be Biblical submission. Over the years, I've gotten the pat on the back, the thanks, all the attention, and she has been Bette Midler's "face without a name." How incredibly humbling to be joined to a Godly, submissive wife!

But men, your wife cannot eagerly submit to someone who doesn't deserve respect. Respect must be earned! How is that done? As Jesus earned the respect of the church, He died for her! And Jesus didn't just die physically, He also died to self-will. Dying physically is not as bad for some as dying to self-will. "Like a city whose walls are broken down is a man who lacks self control." (Prov 25:28 NIV). A city whose walls are broken down is a city under threat of siege. It lay unprotected and vulnerable to all sorts of threats. Likewise, a family where a husband lacks self-control is vulnerable to a siege by the enemy.

These are men who put down their wives, both publicly and privately, and end up piercing their own souls. I know of a man who hasn't had a home made peach pie for over 40 years, because 40 years ago he repeatedly, albeit jokingly, mocked his wife's pie, embarrassing her to near tears at a work social. Words wound, and are impossible to retract, being somewhat like putting toothpaste back into the tube you just squeezed it out of.

Some men lack self-control with their money. They sabotage the family income by giving in freely to recreational spending, or for that whim item they couldn't live without. They don't realize that self-control with their money builds a trusting, reassuring environment for the family. There's not that threat of not making the payment because of out of place spending. A man who spends on his wife before himself builds trust into that area of the relationship.

A man with self-control resolves conflicts quickly. He does not let it burn inside: "In your anger do not sin; do not let the sun go down while you are still angry, and do not give the devil a foothold." (Eph 4:26–27 NIV). My wife and I have had some late nights, and early mornings, but I cannot rest until I know in my heart that a conflict is resolved. Apologies must be offered, and a good relationship is made of both parties who are striving to initialize it: "If possible, so far as it depends on you, be at peace with all men." (Rom 12:18 NASB).

A self-controlled man understands fidelity, and will protect his heart from wandering away from his vows: "Let your fountain be blessed, And rejoice in the wife of your youth." (Prov 5:18 NASB). He remembers the covenant he embraced. He remembers to what and to whom he vowed fidelity. That man realizes that his vows were made in the presence of witnesses and before an omnipresent God who should be respectfully feared: "When a man makes a vow to the LORD or takes an oath to obligate himself by a pledge, he must not break his word but must do everything he said." (Num 30:2 NIV). And again: "If you make a vow to the LORD your God, do not be slow to pay it, for the LORD your God will certainly demand it of you and you will be guilty of sin." (Deu 23:21 NIV).

I've heard married men speak of women as "art," implying that as art they can be admired and goggled. But men do not give themselves to art in the same way they give themselves to a beautiful woman. Let not anything steal for even a second the place that only a wife should have in your relationship. Fight the temptation to wander and lust. A man who finds it easy to wander and lust after promising vows to a wife will likewise find it easy to wander and lust after promising vows to God.

My college professor of Old Testament Studies pointed out an interesting component of vows. The word covenant, or vow, is translated from the Aramaic "*berith*", which means literally "a cutting."[45] The covenant cutting was a practice the ancient Hebrews knew quite well. It was part of agreements and promises. In Abram's covenant with God, both Abram and God passed through the pieces of a heifer, goat, and ram that had been cut in two and laid opposite one another.[46] As Dr. Merrill said, "Between them passed God and Abram symbolically, the total effect suggesting the binding of God and Abram together in a blood relationship the nature of which would lend to the covenant promise a certain unconditional indissolubility."[47]

Envision the following scenario in the transaction of property in which there were certain commitments and promises made by the two parties. To seal the vow, an animal was slain and cut into parts. The various parts were then arranged along a path that both parties would walk. As they walked along the path, and among the pieces of cut up animal, they would repeat the words of the agreement they hade made. They might say: "In the presence of God, I promise to give you this property for your fifteen hundred shekels of silver. If I fail to uphold my vow before God, then let Him do to me what we have done to this animal." My point being, that vows are to be taken seriously! Flirtation and seeing others as "art" denigrates the marriage vow!

Just as God announced the curse, He also announced the

cure. The wonderful thing to remember is that we can rebuke the curse on our marriages by following the principles God has outlined. The fact is, either we live harmoniously as husband and wife, or, face the affliction of a hindered relationship with God. Isn't that what Peter meant when he said: "grant her honor as a fellow heir of the grace of life, so that your prayers may not be hindered." (cf. 1 Pet 3:7). Or again, from the prophet Malachi: "Another thing you do: You flood the Lord's altar with tears. You weep and wail because he no longer pays attention to your offerings or accepts them with pleasure from your hands. {14} You ask, "Why?" It is because the LORD is acting as the witness between you and the wife of your youth, because you have broken faith with her, though she is your partner, the wife of your marriage covenant. (Mal 2:13–14 NIV).

We are asking God to allow calamity if we fail to keep our vows! In a day of broken contracts and loose tongued promises, we need men of moral integrity who can take the hand of their bride from her father, and cherish her with the same respect and love that he does. Will you take this woman to be your wife? Those are words to be considered. They are not to be taken lightly or unadvisedly. If you have taken this woman, where have you taken her?

Let me end this in brutal transparency. I want to quote to you a portion of a letter written to me by my wife while I was away on internship thirty-one years ago. I've saved it these many years for it's a strange treasure to my heart. It is a reminder of my failure, a plea to do better in my relationship with her, and an admonition to cherish the one God has given me. She writes: "As I sit here this morning, I am thinking of how much I love you. Doesn't it seem strange that we are scrappy a lot of the time that we are together? It seems trite to say that maybe things will be better after we get away from school, but, I sincerely hope that our both working full time for the Lord does make a difference."

My wife and I have both carried into our relationship hidden closets full of hurts and abuses from our childhood. At times, we unwittingly press a wrong button that prods some of those hurts and abuses like a sharp needle into raw flesh. Defensive, careless, counter-comments are made, and emotions are left dangling dangerously close to collapse. Through the years we have found only one Healer for our emotional nausea.

God has used the pains of those moments to make within me a pathway to Himself. After thirty-six years of marriage, that pathway is well worn, used often in times of repentance from a sharp word spoken, or attitude taken. Because of our "one flesh," the cruel arrows thrust out from me to her, have ended up piercing my own heart! I am humble, broken really, by her meekness and willingness to forgive. She is like a sheep who is gathered back to her shepherd after he has been unusually unkind. Nestling her head into his lap, she looks up with saucer brown eyes, and calls in a gentle "BAAA, I love you." That well worn path of prayer has led to a place of surrender. It has led me towards self-sacrifice, love, and forgiveness. It has become a place of wisdom and better understanding.

Relationships must be worked at. People don't stay together because of what the world calls "love." That love is almost always based on something external. In the end it doesn't last. The outside of a person changes, people have accidents, or simply get older. That is what I was trying to tell my son the day my wife misunderstood. I married my wife because I saw in her a "Sarah like" quality. It was her inner beauty I couldn't resist! It is her inner beauty that has never faded, like her gentle spirit and quiet demeanor. It was the qualities my father saw in his wife.

Lest I get in trouble again when she reads this, let me add that my wife has always knocked my socks off! But for me, it is her inner beauty that adds to her outer beauty. She has integrity, and people stay together because a man and woman have the integrity to live by the promises they made before God on their wedding day, and the stamina to follow His ways in their marriage and in their private lives. That's my conviction, and I stand by it!

> Charm is deceptive, and beauty is fleeting;
> but a woman who fears the LORD is to be praised.
> (Prov 31:30 NIV)

"Males Are Meaningless"

Small Group Discussion Questions
Chapter Twelve Review

1. In what ways does a wife reflect her husband's relationship to her?

2. Explain the words "head" and "submission" from both a Biblical and cultural perspective.

3. How can a woman's spouse be her "place" of protection?

4. In what ways can a husband earn respect in his family?

5. Is the appreciation for the anatomy of the human body considered Art by God? What does He mean by saying what He made is good?

6. Have you or your spouse carried a closet full of hurts into your marriage? How do they come out?

Sorry About Wendy's

Sometimes as fathers we make unfortunate decisions that stay as scars upon our lives for a very long time. On one such occasion we were celebrating my youngest son's third birthday. It was our custom to treat our children to their favorite dine-out place in honor of their birthdays. Our youngest son chose to go to McDonald's, and was looking forward to it for days.

It was after church on a Sunday afternoon, I had finished preaching and doing any "touch up" business with members of the congregation I was serving. I was ready for lunch, and so we packed into the car and headed out for the twenty-minute ride to McDonald's. Along the way the little guy whose birthday we were celebrating had fallen sound asleep. The wheels in my head started turning and calculating a way that I could satisfy my craving for carbohydrates, specifically a baked potato with cheese and bacon on it, and, still fulfill my obligation to honor that little guy's birthday wishes.

As we neared our destination, the three-year-old birthday boy was still asleep in the back seat, so I decided to "air" my plans to the rest of the crew. "Suppose we go to Wendy's", I suggested, "We could get salads or baked potatoes, and, they still have hamburgers and fries for our birthday boy." My wife, in her wisdom, suggested I think that plan out better, and, reminded me that our "baby" had insisted on McDonald's, and was looking forward to it for days. Somehow I convinced her and myself that a three-year-old, who was fast asleep in his car seat, would never know the difference between McDonalds and Wendy's. All he really wanted, I persuaded, was a good ole hamburger and French fries, where we got them was not so important. If he were asleep, he would never miss the golden arches, Ronald, or the little nuances that make McDonalds, McDonalds. It seemed like perfect trickery; he could get his hamburger, and, I could get my fill of carbohydrates. He would never know the difference because he would be fast asleep when we drove in.

We parked the car, I un-strapped birthday boy from his car seat, flung him over the shoulder, and carted him inside Wendy's for his promised dinner. Wouldn't you know it, when he awoke he started the questions: "Where are we?" he asked. "We're here to get your birthday hamburger" I responded with enthusiasm. "But, we're not at McDonalds," he insisted, "I thought you promised me we'd go to McDonalds." "Yes", I sputtered, "but look at all the choices you can get here, and plus, I'll take you out for ice cream later." "But, it's not McDonalds," the little guy asserted, "and there's no happy meal."

That day, to my shame, I robbed my little boy of his eagerly anticipated birthday dinner. My son, now grown and in his twenties, still laughingly reminds me of that infamous day from time to time. Who would have known that a three-year-old would know the difference between Wendy's and McDonalds, and, that the incident would be indelibly marked for all his life?

I am so grateful for my son's gracious and Godly forgiveness given me concerning my failure to him as a father. My "driven" selfishness points up a very serious truth about Godly fatherhood and authority in general. There are only two ways to handle authority and power. One is a lie, and leads to disturbing decisions and conclusions, while the other is morally sound, but far more difficult to achieve.

Jesus, talking to His disciples, said: "… You know that those who are considered rulers over the Gentiles lord it over them, and their great ones exercise authority over them. Yet it shall not be so among you; but whoever desires to become great among you shall be your servant. And whoever of you desires to be first shall be slave of all. For even the Son of Man did not come to be served, but to serve, and to give His life a ransom for many." (Mark 10:42 45 NKJV).

I think the "lording over" spoken of by Jesus finds its root in the heart. It is there we succumb to the lie about fatherhood, authority, and leadership. It is there where "rights" take precedent over right. *The New Century Dictionary* defines authority as the "right to command or act."[48] If you buy into that, then I had the right as a father to choose wherever I wanted to go for my son's birthday dinner. In the "Gentile" world it is customary to exercise authority, or lord it over those under your care. But, that is not what Jesus charged us to do.

In His admonition, Jesus re-defined what authority is, totally contradicting the world's "lording over" mentality. For, He says great leadership and example comes from a servant's heart. It is in serving their children and wives that those great husbands and fathers are made.

Men and women of God are formed and hewn out of the spiritual granite of self-sacrifice. It is through surrender of our wills that we begin to touch the essence of God. For, God is love, and, in spite of what the movies tell us, love does have to say "I'm sorry." Love is modeling servanthood, for as Jesus said: "If I then, your Lord and Teacher, have washed your feet, you also ought to wash one another's feet. For I have given you an example, that you should do as I have done to you." (John 13:14 15 NKJV).

I remember an incident during the 1992 Olympics that I was watching on television. The announcers had finished running through the field of athletes for the 400-meter race. They pointed out one American Olympian, Derek Redmond, who was a standout performer. He held the world record for the event, but, in spite of all his accomplishments, he had never won the gold. Having won all the previous heats leading up to the big race, it seemed like this day was a strong possibility for Derek to do that.

I was watching the participants go through the last turn, and head for the final stretch to the finish line, when the announcer, in disbelief, announced: "Redmond is down!" At first, no one seemed to know what was going on. Was he tripped? Or did he fall because of injury?

As the television camera shot the scene, a man came running up to Derek, having forced his way through the crowd and security officials. I guessed that it was probably his trainer, but then, instead of seeing to his injures, he placed his shoulder under his arm, helped him stand to his feet, and walked with him across the finish line, just a few yards away. I remember the stands exploding in cheers, standing to their feet. The man turned out to be his father, and the world watched in amazement as both father and son completed the race together.

This story could focus on the father. He was the one who loved his son so much that he broke through the stands, fought his way around security, and accompanied him for the rest of the race. But, I'd like to put you in the athlete's seat for a minute. The heart of an athlete is determined, expecting to triumph over his opponents every time. His mental determination is only matched by his will to prepare to win. And so, in painstaking surrender, he challenges and forces his body to do things beyond what average bodies can or would want to do.

My daughter-in-law is an accomplished athlete. I am proud of her and her achievements as a student-athlete during her college years. She is an excellent golfer, taught well by her dad and coaches over the years. She too has that aforementioned will and determination to succeed. In her training regimen, she would awaken well before classes and go to the gym, while roommates were still in their beds. There at the gym she would discipline her body by pushing it to the edge, knowing that her next opponent was probably doing the same thing. Finally, she would go to the football stadium where she would run up and down the steep stairs to build up her stamina.

On the course she is focused, knowing what she needs to do to gain victory over her rival. If I were surrounded by the enemy, she is one whom I would put on my backside without hesitation. She has the heart of an athlete.

Now imagine what Derek Redmond was feeling as he sprawled out in pain on the track. All those years of preparing his mind and body for the Olympics had resulted in a blown out Achilles tendon. Not only was he facing the end of the Olympics, but a career. Athletes are proud, and want to finish the course on their own. Yet, Derek willingly took the hand of his father, propped his crumbled body on his shoulder, and hobbled towards the finish line. Broken in body and spirit, Derek finished the course of the greatest event of his life, but it was not the Olympics. That day, through the surrender of his will, he swallowed his pride, and won more than the gold medal offered to athletes. He won the admiration of his father!

There are times that the unexpected and unforeseen tragedies of life cause us to crumble to the most important track of our lives. We fail at fatherhood, or, some other type of leadership, and are faced with what we know are costly injuries. We too have a father, an ultimate Father in heaven, who comes to our aide to help. Like Derek, we are faced with a decision: do we reach up to accept the strong "hand" reaching out to us, or do we in self preservation and pride determine we need no help? It takes the surrender of our wills to admit that we are not the fathers, husbands, or leaders we ought to be, but, self sacrifice and admission of our wounds begins the molding process for making example setters. Then we will become men who are like spring water that has been forced through many feet of hard ground and rock, becoming purified as it reaches its final destination, and finally we will be useful to the spiritually thirsty that we encounter.

Like Derek's father, God has a final destination purpose for our lives. It doesn't matter that we come in first, or even are among the best, only that we succeed: "… let us also lay aside every encumbrance, and the sin which so easily entangles us, and let us run with endurance the race that is set before us, fixing our eyes on Jesus, the author and perfecter of faith …" (Heb 12:12 NASB).

I've come to realize that leadership isn't taken, but accepted. For that reason, it needs to be developed. We were having dinner at a local restaurant with a neighbor couple that we know. They're a young family with a little boy and girl. As I watched daddy at the restaurant, I was reminded of earlier days and similar settings with our children.

As daddy's girl sank her fingers into her spaghetti plate, the tomato sauce oozed all through her little hands and eventually ended up on her face. It looked pretty hopeless to me, but daddy gave the admonition anyway: "Sweetie, use the napkin" he pleaded as he handed her the cloth from the table. It was a thought that had never entered her mind, and, attempts to use it only seemed to make matters worse, smearing the sauce everywhere.

On the way home, daddy and I were enjoying a peaceful, thoughtful conversation. Then came the intense cry from the back of the van: "Daddy, pull over, I have to use the bathroom." "But son," protested his father, "there are no businesses through here, and, we're just a few minutes from home." "But I have to go now" called the anxious little voice from the back, "I can't wait!" Daddy tried one more desperate attempt to stall off the situation: "I have to go too," he said, "but I'm a big boy and can wait a few minutes till we get home." At that point mommy stepped in: "Honey," she said, "his bladder isn't as big as yours!" In surrender daddy eventually pulled the van off the road, where he shaded the body of his young son from the dozens of homes in the area. I loved what I was seeing, a young man being carved into a father by the "tools" of God.

Our neighbor daddy was being refined. There will be many more messy dinners at restaurants, and many more roadside stops for emptying bladders while God is making a selfless leader, a mentor to his family, a daddy who will give his very life. He is a man in the process of learning patience and surrender, which will lead one day to the heartbreak of release. My young neighbor friend is being preened to leave a heritage of faith to his children.

Fathers develop as they stay under God's tutelage, and wise fathers do as God suggests: "Fix these words of mine in your hearts and minds; tie them as symbols on your hands and bind them on your foreheads. Teach them to your children, talking about them when you sit at home and when you walk along the road, when you lie down and when you get up." (Deu 11:18 19 NIV).

My wife and I attended a church nearby, as we waited for our next assignment from God. We attended for nearly a year, and almost every week we would pass by a teenage couple on our way to our seats. I usually stopped, hoping for a little small talk, but after a smile, handshake, and pat on the back there were normally few words made between us. After all, what would a teenage couple and a couple in their fifties have in common?

But then, there was this fascinating day at church. We had just had a powerful worship experience and several of us joined at the front of the church for prayer. I hadn't realized that our teenaged friends were there as well. They had been praying hand in hand on their knees. When they stood to their feet, I reached out to give the young man a hug. To my surprise, he held on in deep embrace. It was real! As this young man buried his head into my shoulder, tears oozing like soul blood, I somehow felt "weakened" by humility and wonder. I realized as he held his grip, that to him I was not just another adult body, he felt that he was embracing a friend. Before returning to our seats, he asked if I would be his mentor! The little "touches" we had been offering to them as we passed by every Sunday morning had produced a silent bond between us.

Greg Norman, the professional golfer, seemingly has it all

together on the golf course. He shows little emotion during play, as he strolls from hole to hole with a tough exterior. In 1996 Norman was leading in the masters, holding a 6-stroke lead in the final round. But, the lead melted away as Nick Faldo came on strong. The tournament was finalized on the last hole, when Faldo pulled off the win. This is what *Sports Illustrated* said: "Now, as Faldo made one last thrust into Norman's heart with a 15-foot birdie putt on the 72nd hole, the two of them came toward each other, Norman trying to smile, looking for a handshake and finding himself in the warmest embrace instead. As they held that hug, held it even as both of them cried, Norman changed just a little. 'I wasn't crying because I'd lost,' Norman said the next day. '… I've lost a lot of golf tournaments. I'll lose a lot more. I cried because I'd never felt that from another man before. I've never had a hug like that in my life.'"[49]

Referring to Norman's emotionless demeanor, Rick Reilly said, "It's the way of his stoic father, and he had learned it begrudgingly. 'I used to see my father, getting off a plane or something, and I'd want to hug him,' he recalled once. 'But he'd only shake my hand.'"[50] Kind of sad isn't it? The one man whose hug would have meant more than all the golfing championships his son competed in never knew what it was like to be welcomed home by the warm embrace of a grateful child. How easy it would have been, nothing needed to be said, no awkward embarrassing words, just a hug around a very appreciative neck. That man never knew that the emotions of his son would one day be expressed in the arms of a competitor.

Sometimes it's those unspoken things that give the greatest examples. Fatherhood, like servanthood, is finding that last bit of energy when in exhaustion you return home from work to find your three year old wanting to have a "horsy back ride." It's recording the ball game on television in order to have a family picnic. Fatherhood is when we show our children how much we love their mother by how we honor her. It's in giving proper respect to all in the family unit. It is character, dignity, and integrity at all times. It is to suffer personally and sometimes privately for doing what is right: "…if you suffer for doing good and you endure it, this is commendable before God. To this you were called, because Christ suffered for you, leaving you an example, that you should follow in his steps." (1 Pet 2:20 21 NIV). That is all done with very little words, but never by a man who is self-centered.

There is no equal to the abuse of the self-centered moral fiber in our society. I was there when a mother blaringly berated her hardened son, calling him stupid and no good because he did something she didn't like. I've listened to the stories my wife told of a father who gave her up, only to adopt another little girl to sit on his knee when he visited her. I've sat across from the young lady soaked in tears, holding her head between her hands, telling me of the several times she had aborted babies, each one tearing at a piece of her spirit.

It's the same lie of the "Gentile" world that Jesus spoke about. You don't need to serve, just be served it says. Don't take into account what others feel, say, or care. It's a choice of leadership that you can take, but beware of the disturbing consequences. It is encouraging by its example a society of self-preservers, those raised without the pattern of leaning on the shoulder of a heavenly Father to help them across the finish line of life.

Share your life, live real, but also, say it with words. I can remember my father attending every one of my little league baseball games. When I advanced from the lower division to the higher league, my father was excited for me. I was a pretty good pitcher in the lower division, but, there were plenty of good pitchers in the higher league, and so, because I was an all around decent player, they played me in the field.

I heard the crack of the bat, as the ball floated lazily toward me in center field. I was playing deep, and the ball was losing altitude quickly. It was all up to me. I had to make a quick decision whether to play it on the hop and let it be a hit, or, to lunge after it for the out. I hesitated indecisively, just for a fraction of a second, but it was enough to ruin the play. I lunged with all I had, gearing to make the play, and to take us out of the treacherous inning, but instead came up with air. As I tumbled awkwardly out of control, I watched as the ball rolled out from behind me toward the fence.

I'll never forget how I felt at that moment. I had been a star player in the lower leagues, but now, I had made a huge gaffe that had cost my team dearly. I was embarrassed, humiliated before the stands of people, and knew that my father had been watching. In shame, I approached my father after the game; I just wanted to leave the ball field as quickly as possible. I was riding home in the darkness of my blunder, fighting back the tears, wanting to be alone, when out of nowhere my father said: "What a great play! You almost made a perfect shoestring catch. You missed it by mere inches, but, you did the right thing, and, your effort was absolutely outstanding."

What my father perhaps did not know was I needed his words more than anything that night. When he spoke those words into my broken spirit, it didn't matter so much what anyone else thought, for I had the approbation needed from the one who knew me the closest. Baseball was my avenue to emotional normalcy, and about the only thing in life that I felt very good at. I was a misfit at school, and socially underprivileged, but I knew that I could play baseball. Baseball was the world where I was equal or better than anyone else. When that which dignified me as a person came crashing down, my father was there sharing his life with me, embracing me near to his heart, and, revealing his compassion through words.

If my father were there when I made the blunder with my son on his birthday, I imagine he would have said the same thing again: "Son, you missed it by inches. You were almost there, you love your son, you truly want to be a good father, but you allowed the self to get in the way. Don't give up, another opportunity will come." My father started a pattern for our family, and it is that selfless and sincere heritage of my father that I wish to pass along to my children, and, to many generations after. For those of us siblings that knew him well, my father is not merely remembered, he is missed, missed for his Biblical content, unconditional love, and his example of selflessness.

> "When I was a boy in my father's house,
> still tender... he taught me and said,
> 'Lay hold of my words with all your heart;
> keep my commands and you will live.'"
> (Prov 4:3 4 NIV).

"Males Are Meaningless"

Small Group Discussion Questions
Chapter Thirteen Review

1. In what ways does Jesus' definition of great leadership as servanthood affect fatherhood?

2. How would servant hood relate to discipline?

3. In what specific ways does God use the family to refine us?

4. Name some unspoken acts that would show appreciation, love, or respect. Can you think of an example that showed you that?

5. How has God used failure to be a part of your life? How about verbal encouragement?

6. How has God given you approval or esteem at a time that His opinion was what you really needed? How does that relate to fatherhood?

The Road Less Traveled

Two roads diverged in a wood, and I—
I took the one less traveled by,
And that has made all the difference.[51]

There was once a woman who fell in love and got married. It was a wonderful wedding, with several guests. She wore a beautiful pristine white dress. As the years went by, she and her husband had the typical three children, two boys and a girl. All seemed to be well, with the white picket fence and rose garden out back.

But times were tough, and her husband had to work late on many occasions figuring the extra income would come in handy. It all happened so innocently, a few friends had come in for dinner, and at the last minute her husband called, having to work late again. Conversation went well, especially with the man making eye contact with her. She knew he was recently separated from his wife. How did that happen? He seems like such a nice guy.

A few months later, another special occasion that her husband couldn't attend, and there they meet again. Face to face, laughing together, having a genuinely good time, what could be wrong with this? The conversation turned a bit, from laughing and good times to early morning tired discussion. They spoke of relationships, disappointments, and hopes for the future. How closely their dreams aligned.

"I'll be in town tomorrow morning," he says, "let's get a cup of coffee." It's only coffee. "Sure," she says, and the morning sun is met by a doorbell. He's there, looking a bit more handsome than before, her husband is still on the business trip. "Come in," she says, "we may as well make the coffee here."

The story has been told a million times, one thing led to another, the two end up together, naked and ashamed. She has cheated, strangely for reasons she can't quite put her finger on. The result is not expected, she feels dirty, defiled, and unworthy of her husband.

After several months, she is still unable to cope with the shame and guilt of what she has done. Her husband is aware, he has asked for a separation, but even more crushing is the look, or lack thereof, on his face, for she has broken everything within this man. He no longer has the gumption to get up, to face another day. She no longer can stand to see him like this.

So secretly, on a morning the family should be going to church, she leaves her three children and husband still sleeping in their beds. Having put aside enough money for a ticket, she hops a plane heading for the opposite coast. A couple of years pass by so slowly, she barely remembers the warm bed and rose garden that were once hers.

Not only that, but feeling so much like a tramp made it easy to become one. After all, she had already destroyed everything that meant so much to her. But what a shame, don't you think? She had exchanged freedom for a certain type of slavery, not the binding of one's hands and feet, but even greater, the bondage in one's heart.

And so she worked as a prostitute, getting jobs from the "man." He was considerate at first, almost understanding of all she had been through. The loneliness, emptiness, and guilt subsided from time to time while in his "care." But it didn't last, and the abuse began to flow when he thought she could do better. It wasn't so much the slaps and punches that bothered her, after all, she was mostly doped up anyway, but it was the wounds that never had enough anesthetic to erase them, those mental wounds that reminded her of what she was. The "man" would never let her forget she was now a drug addicted whore!

In the meantime, her ex-husband still hard at work, mostly now to keep his mind occupied, again had to take another of his infamous business trips. He arrived early on a Tuesday morning, in time to catch a bus downtown and grab a bite to eat for breakfast. Sitting in the booth, drinking his coffee, he noticed the commotion. Just outside the little café a scuffle was going on between a man and woman. Why wasn't anyone coming to her rescue? The streets are filling with people by now, surely someone will intervene. He watches the backhands being delivered, opening up gaping cuts on her lips. The man grabs her by the hair, yanks her to the ground, and starts kicking her in the side. What has she done? Who is this woman? Why is she here on the streets so early in the morning?

He can't continue his breakfast; the scene going on outside has robbed him of his appetite. He realizes he must turn away, but catches a glimpse of her bloodied face. She has a strange sort of attraction to him, though he can't quite get a good look at her. She's standing there with bowed head, as if shamed by some unspeakable act that must have happened in her life. There she is, exposed to the crowd, disheveled, dirty, and barely clothed. With an enigmatic sense of urgency the traveling business man feels he must find out more about this strangely attractive woman. What's her name? Where does she come from? Why is she being slapped around on the open street, and nobody seems to care.

Can it be? He decides to leave the café and join the crowd now forming outside. It is then that many of his questions are answered. One bystander says: "She's nothing but a used up whore! Been on the streets here a good two years. Look at her skinny disgusting body, I'll bet she's loaded with STD's." "Yes," says another onlooker, "the city needs to do something about having trash like this on the streets." Most of the other male onlookers are speaking in disgust, but none can keep their eyes off her. The business man is surprised by all he hears. Could it be? Once again his mind wanders into distant thoughts, only to be abruptly interrupted by the harsh voice of the man kicking at the woman, "You owe me money," he says, "you're into me big time and I'm gonna collect one way or another."

The street conversation continues: "I heard she used to be married," says one. Married? The business man considers that for a moment. His brain is flooded with even more questions. There must have been a time for her when things were better. If she were married, someone must have fallen in love with her, and she had fallen in love with him. What a shame, he thinks, that this battered, used woman once had a wedding day. She probably wore a white dress, signifying her innocence; she must have pledged her life to another, to stay with him until death. She would have thrown a bouquet of flowers to cheering onlook-ers, and left with a husband, rushing down the front stairs of a church in a hail of rice, reaching the car waiting to wisp them away on a honeymoon, and a life that would be happy forever-more. Together they would make a home, talk of days to come, and maybe even buy a house with a yard, where they could grow flowers and walk along a path holding hands. She had once been held in the passionate embrace of a loving husband. She was cared for, supported, had a decent roof over her head, and a warm bed to sleep in at night.

But now, all of that has faded for her, and things have come to this, to this street, to this moment, to this abuse of the pimp now beating on her. Now, she was shamed, having spent the last couple of years enslaved to a man making a living at her expense, and to the pills she originally took to ease the mental anguish, because she considered herself trash, just pure trash!

Again, the business man's thoughts are broken by the same voice on the street: "I was told she had three children that she left behind. Three children and a husband, can you imagine that?" The traveling business man is captured yet again by the thoughts and images swirling around in his brain, and his mind wanders into the distance. Could it be? Being there on the streets that day by "chance," merely because a co-worker had gotten sick, he was suddenly overcome with passion towards this broken, battered, nearly naked woman that the crowd was pointing at in disgust. Indeed, could it be? The situation felt familiar to him, and plied against the raw feelings that had settled just under the surface of his hardened stone exterior. He too was once happily married, he too knew the warm embrace of a loving spouse who had given him three children, and he too had been divorced!

By now, the morning sun was beginning to peep out above the tall downtown buildings. The pimp on the street was still raging, because the woman wasn't worth a thing to him any longer, and he just wanted revenge for his lost money. The crowd was beginning to disperse, everybody had someplace to be, and this woman just wasn't worth worrying about; she was just one of many. The feeling of most was that she was getting exactly what she deserved. It was her choice to have left her husband and kids. It was her choice to go out into the streets as a common harlot and sell her body to anyone willing. Why would anyone help such a no-good tramp like this?

Just then a nearby religious fanatic breaks through the crowd. He's holding a brick in his hand: "I'll tell you what they used to do," he shrieks, hurling the brick ruthlessly towards the battered woman at the center of commotion. The brick finds its mark, heartlessly gashing her forehead with a deep open wound.

It was then, her head being flailed backward by the force of the brick, that the traveling man caught his first short glimpse of her face. Could it be? Take away the dirt, the bloodied cheeks, the years of abuse written into her drug withered skin, and yes, it could be. His heart pounded within him, he couldn't take the chance to let her go! Frantically he searched his wallet for every bit of cash. He counts out to the pimp, one by one, ten one hundred dollar bills, then reaches for the expensive Patek Philippe watch he was wearing on his wrist. Everything he had!

The crowd is stunned! Their shock is obvious, as silence falls upon them like a sheet being wrapped around a baby going to sleep. The pimp's jawbones drop, as he stares in disbelief of what he is being offered. Every head in the crowd turns toward this traveling man. One thousand bucks and a Patek Philippe watch, easily worth another fifty grand? Is he nuts? The traveling man is now standing before this woman, his outstretched hands dripping with the money that he is offering to the pimp. In haste the pimp accepts the offer, handing the tired, battered, broken woman over to the stranger in the street.

But, the woman on the street has never lifted her head. So far as she knows this is just another stranger who would take her, use her, maybe even abuse her, and ultimately cast her aside. She expects to be treated as usual, with a tight hand around the wrist, and a rough yank that would pull her down the street in shame, in front of the gathered crowd. She had no light inside, it had dimmed years ago, when she had given up her warm bed, three children, and a husband who cared, in exchange for the slavery of the streets. She had no reason to hope or dare believe that she would be treated in any other way but like the swine she now felt she was.

But instead, this incredible thing happens. The traveling man gently reaches for her hand and leads the dishonored woman slowly away from the crowd. Down the street they walk, her hand in his, while onlookers are whispering ridiculous things to one another. Who knows what they expected to see? The man rounded a distant corner far enough away from the peering crowd, and paused in the middle of an alley. Then, he gently cupped her face in his hands, wiping the tears away with his thumb, and lifted her head to meet his eyes. "Gomer," he softly whispers, then repeats, "Gomer." Where had she heard that gentle voice before? How long has it been since someone has called her by her right name, and with such tenderness?

She opened her eyes to discover the face of Hosea, her former husband, her once devoted lover. After years of abuse and shame, she is now being held in his strong arms as he continues to softly say: "Gomer, I'm setting you free." Tears once more well up in her eyes and make their way slowly down her filthy cheeks. As they touch her cracked lips they burn with the taste of salt, like the poison from the years of abuse being washed from her heart. She ponders Hosea's words again. "Free," that word had long since lost its meaning to her, in more ways than one.

"Free," she finally manages under trembling breath, "free." "Yes," Hosea says, "you are free to go wherever you want." I need to pause here in the story. It seems a bit unrealistic, don't you think? What spouse would so easily welcome back a partner who deliberately broke vows? What spouse would want to take back a partner riddled with STD's, the "scars" left in memory of rampant sin? It would take a kind of love difficult to understand wouldn't it? As you ponder that, I'm telling you it's the point of this book. Read on.

Gomer can hardly believe her fate. She knows she is unworthy of such reconciliation, and meekly speaks those simple words that Hosea longed to hear: "I want to go home!" With those words Hosea responds with a sentence captured forever in the pages of Scripture: "Then I told her, 'You are to live with me many days; you must not be a prostitute or be intimate with any man, and I will live with you.'" (Hosea 3:3 NIV). That very day Hosea took Gomer, his disloyal love, back home, not with condemnation or ulterior motives, he just took her home as his wife.

Hosea chapters one through three tells the amazing story of God's love in a way that every human being can comprehend. Hosea is a picture of God. He had fallen in love with an adulteress who refused to stay faithful. After three children they were divorced, and settled into different markets. He apparently maintained his farming, while she worked as a prostitute. Hosea runs across her one day, and a surge of love is met by God's direction to take her back. Hosea buys her back with fifteen shekels of silver and ten bushels of barley.

God, through Hosea, is making a point to you and me. Like the adulteress Gomer was married to Hosea, we too with adulterous tendencies are married to God, and we too wander and lust after the world around us. Just as Hosea purchased the freedom of his love, so God has purchased us back from the hands of the "pimp," out of slavery to the world, with a gut wrenching move that cost Him the life of His Son on Calvary. It was the best He had to give and it was everything that He could give! Hosea reminds us that our continued "spiritual adultery" not only breaks the law of God, it breaks the heart of God. Love is one attribute of God we can partially understand. We all crave love, and, conversely, we all can relate to the pain of having that love adulterated. That's been the message of this book. There are many of us in the Christian arena who are dangerously close to spiritual adultery. God has taken us back once, and it is our accountability to remain loyal to Him. Remember the powerful admonition from James: "You adulterous people, don't you know that friendship with the world is hatred toward God?" (James 4:4a NIV). I want to conclude with four thoughts.

Spiritual Choices

We are constantly faced with choices. They direct our lives, and are the most important facet of life. Our choices determine how educated we will be, where we will gain income, or even how healthy our bodies are. All of those choices are important, but not critical. The critical choice involves our spirituality. What we choose to believe about life determines our legacy and destiny at death.

My father helped me to see a very valuable truth. His life was not about gaining money, fame, or power. Being trapped by the lie of that lifestyle is like becoming a slave to its curse, the gradual drawing in of one's spirit to desire more, bigger, and better things. In my father, I witnessed a man who had nothing, exchange it for everything of value. When he died at the age of fifty-four, his legacy was not bank accounts, houses, or land, but, because of his choices, he has successfully passed down to his children, the key to finding real "richness."

I recently found a letter he wrote back in 1951 to the now defunct *Herald Of Life* magazine. It reads in part: "We feel so wonderful since we have taken Jesus into our home. We always thought our home was happy, but we now realize we had nothing before Christ... Our lives were incomplete. Since we have five children we thought it was too inconvenient to go to church, but we find it very easy to do now and really look forward to it." That was fifty-five years ago, and the start of my own spiritual heritage, for I was then two, and the youngest of those five children he mentioned. Be reminded, lest you feel our present day schedules prevent us from making such choices, that my father worked at a punishing job in a foundry for six full days a week, yet, he was determined to give his family a spiritual background on his day off.

One thing I realized over the years as I watched my father was that he didn't make his choices out of desperation, but in spite of desperation. When the unpredictable desperation occurred, as it did so often in our meager conditions, he had already determined to have a mindset that followed hard after God. That choice drew him into a deeper association and communication with his God. His freedom from the desperate situations in his life was the direct result of his enslavement to Christ.

Thom Shumate sings a beautiful song written by Michael

Cody called "Freedom, Love, and Forgiveness." In the song, Abraham Lincoln buys a young slave girl off the auction block. He unlocks the chains, and begins walking with her down a busy southern avenue. People are shocked at the sight, but old Abe doesn't seem to care. Instead, he turns to the girl, looks her in the eyes, and says "Young lady you are free." In response, the young slave girl gazes into the sky and asks, "What does that word mean?" "Can I say whatever I want to say?" "Yes," Abe answers, "you can say whatever you want to say." She asks again, "Can I do whatever I want to do?" And, again Abe answers "Yes, you can do whatever you want to do." Then, she presses on, "Can I go wherever I want to go?" Once more Abe responds, "You can go wherever you want to go." By now, the street is buzzing with people pointing and whispering to one another, as the girl in humility and thankfulness says to old Abe, "Then what I want to say, and what I want to do, is go with you."[52]

That song reminds me of my father. I saw in him a man filled with appreciation and humility towards the One who set him free through a healing relationship. The One who set my father free from the tangled distortion of false hope, false happiness, and false security, is the One he wanted to go with throughout his life.

The Bible makes the point that we are all going to be indentured to one of two things, we will either be devoted to the world, in which case we become its slave, or we will be devoted and enslaved to Christ. That which we devote our lives to will become our focal point of worship, and eventual surrender of all we are. Worship involves intimacy without reservation, a sense of nakedness and exposure before that which is worshipped. It stakes a claim upon our soul that unveils who, what, and why we are.

In the Garden of Eden, when mankind was surrendered to God, they worshipped Him "naked and not ashamed." But notice, after the fall they were exposed before the world and ashamed before God, because, their worship changed focus from the things of God to the things of the world.

When one feels he has found the "secret" of success and happiness in the things of this world, he will soon worship his "findings," for by them he reasons that he lives in luxury and enjoys the choicest things. Jesus, knowing the debilitation of being enslaved and naked to the world offers this: "Come to me, all you who are weary and burdened and I will give you rest. Take my yoke upon you and learn from me, for I am gentle and humble in heart, and you will find rest for your souls. For my yoke is easy and my burden is light." (Mat 11:28 30 NIV).

The point is, you will be yoked to something. You have no choice about enslavement, but you can choose what you want to be enslaved by! That is the offer Jesus set before us, either "His yoke," or the world's yoke. Being enslaved to the world's trappings is a maddening, chaotic never ending stirring of our soul for more, but our Maker offers an alternative "rest for our soul."

There must be more than desperation that leads you to a hunger after God. Historically, the people of God have proved time and again that desperation alone does not bring you closer to Him. When Israel left Egypt they were running from a powerful army that outnumbered them by the multitudes. They ran as far and as hard as they could, until they came dead into the face of the Red Sea. Seeing the clouds of dust being raised by the Egyptian chariots nipping at their rear quarters, the Israelites, in desperation, called upon God for help and deliverance. In a powerful display of the miraculous, God split the Red Sea, dividing the water into two walls, making a dry pathway for the Israelites to cross over. The Egyptian army, attempted to do the same thing, but instead, was sucked under by the walls of water that suddenly collapsed upon them.

The incident was remarkable in the eyes of those there that day, and they took the time to worship with respect and adoration the God who delivered them out of slavery and near death. The moment was pressed into the history of Israel, being passed from generation to generation by word of mouth, and chronicled into the pages of Scripture. But, moments of desperation are forgotten, and shortly thereafter we read of these same people of God making a golden calf idol to worship saying: "…This is your god, O Israel, who brought you up from the land of Egypt." (Exo 32:4 NASB).

Old timers refer to a "fox hole" religion, a term used to describe the acts of repentance and promises of faithfulness that were uttered up to God in desperation during the first and second world wars, as soldiers sitting in dug out fortresses cringed while bullets whizzed by just a few feet overhead. But when danger passed, so did the memory of commitment and allegiance to God.

Healthy relationships are born out of intimacy, not desperation. Imagine you and your spouse enjoying a romantic walk along the beach. Hand in hand you share memories that just the two of you have created together. Attempting to draw out the love language that pleases the palate of your ears, you ask, "Why did you marry me?" Your spouse, looking deeply into your eyes, answers: "Because I was desperate." There is obviously something wrong with that picture, and, there is likewise something wrong with one's attempt to have a relationship with God based on desperation only.

It is through intimacy and discovery that relationship with God is birthed and even further nurtured. It is when one intimately surrenders the complexities of his life to the Master, that the Master's faithfulness is tested, tried, and proven. That in return leads to a discovery that the One who knows all and sees all, also controls all. My father's life situations tested and proved the faithfulness of God time and again to both himself and his children.

My father had a deep appreciation for the mercy given to him from a God that cared for him in spite of his social, economical, and, more importantly, spiritual depravities. That discovery set him free from the inside out! Just like the slave girl looking up to old Abe, he cried from the depths of his heart to his Rescuer: "What I want to say, and what I want to do, is go with You."

We have a wonderful golden retriever dog named Cody that we got after my wife and I became empty nesters. Cody arrived at our house when he was just about six weeks old. We're pretty much the only "family" he remembers being a part of. We brought him into our home, shared with him our bed, fed him from our hands, and took him just about everywhere we went. He'll ride and sit in the car for hours, just to be with the "pack" that he feels part of. At times we feel guilty because he has to wait in the car for such long periods of time as we shop, eat, or whatever.

You'd think he would remember those rough times, and have a second thought about wanting to come along with us everywhere we go, but that just isn't the case. He listens carefully to our conversations to catch word clues of what's going on. If we accidentally interject words involving "car", "truck", "shoes", or "go" into our conversation, then he gets immediately on point to watch our every move. If we start heading towards a door, he stands on his hindquarters, grabs us by the waist with his front paws, and hangs on for his life. At ninety-five pounds, he is resolute! If we're going somewhere, then he's going too.

It doesn't matter that the last time out he was waiting for hours in the back seat of a car, Cody just wants to be with his "pack." It is his quest for intimacy that pushes him through the tough times of waiting in the car. Sometimes he's rewarded by getting a walk in the park, sometimes not, but the reward is not essential, it is mere gravy added to the intimacy. Cody's incentive is for intimacy, nothing more and nothing less, for him there is no other alternative but to go where we go.

And so it was for my father. It didn't seem to matter that his world was perceived by others to be destitute of resources, or that his living conditions appeared to lack relative pleasure. No, as bumpy as his ride was, he just wanted to go with his "Freedom Maker." He considered no other alternative but to follow hard after Jesus, the love of his life, and nothing would deter him from a truthful life or tempt him toward dishonest gain. Though tough times came and passed, and he steadfastly maintained a straightforward walk with his Master. He was a blessed man, not because of what he owned, but because of what owned him. He held tightly to the portals of faith with a conviction that put the things of God first in his life. Those are the things, in the end that are worth giving your life to, for they are bound to be replicated in the lives of those who love you.

Morality

My second thought involves morality. Perhaps the memories I have written about my father remind you of someone similar in your life, someone who held on to values that seemed unremarkable by the world's view of importance. Perhaps they are someone whose honor could be trusted with a word and a handshake; someone whose life you subconsciously admire and respect; someone in the past, long since forgotten in the world, but always alive in the most serious decision-making processes you make, those times when you ask, what are the things that they would place first in their lives or the things that they would never stray from? They teach us the following lesson.

While it is true that the culture has changed around us, never has moral truth been unable to identify with its present culture. That's the beauty of the Bible, it has always held true throughout the world's changing societies. What was relevant for first century Christians, is likewise relevant to you and me today, and will be relevant long after we have passed. It's an amazing moral truth, with an amazing Author, the likes of which has never been duplicated, and the guts of which will never be eradicated. Therein lies the problem. If moral truth never changes, if God is the same "yesterday, today, and forever," then as Cassius said to Brutus, the fault is "not in our stars, but in ourselves …"[53] Simply put, our moral lives are not because of chance, but because of choice.

There's an interesting story in the Bible that goes like this: there was a famine in the land where Isaac had been living, so he moved to Gerar, an old city near the Mediterranean coast. God gave favor to Isaac so that crops grew well and his herds of animals increased. However, the people in the land he had moved to envied him and maliciously filled the wells that Isaac was using for water with dirt.

Before I finish the story, let me draw a correlation. If you're a Christian in the "land," you are bound to draw the envy of the enemy because of God's favor on your life. As an act of revenge, the enemy will attempt to "fill" certain spiritual wells that you draw life from. Isaac turned his back on the enemy and moved away from them! Now, after he had moved again, this is what the Bible says: "Isaac reopened the wells that had been dug in the time of his father Abraham, which the Philistines had stopped up after Abraham died, and he gave them the same names his father had given them. (Gen 26:18 NIV).

The ancient wells represented an oasis for Israel's nomadic people. There they revived life, both human and animal. There the weary traveler would take a break from the hot desert sun. Abraham was responsible for digging them during his days of travel throughout the area, but, as time passed, the Philistine enemies had stopped them up, rendering them useless.

The moral application is interesting here, for we have fore-fathers who have dug the wells of decency, honor, and integrity before us. Those places are places of relief, in a world where moral decency, honor, and integrity are hard to come by. By those places life is sustained, and, peaceful rest from the scorching rays of the world's influence is found.

Unfortunately, as time passes, our enemy is plugging the wells that were once running more freely than now. It is time for us to think through the values of our hopes and goals, and, perhaps, like Isaac, re-dig the wells that our forefathers painstakingly dug before us. Those are the "wells" of Church attendance, Bible reading and prayer, attention to the family. Those are the "wells" of integrity, honesty, and "doing the right thing." Those are the "wells" of a man's promise kept, a "swearing to his own hurt," a determination to be forthright. We've seen those "wells" eroding before our eyes. Contracts are broken, men break their word, relationships are torn, and little attention is given to the spiritual. And that we are passing to our young! We live in what is now being called by some, the "culture of violence."

The Principle Of Doing

Lisa was standing over the kitchen sink washing dishes. It was a drab morning, the final effects of a stubborn wet weather system that lingered over the area for days. Maybe it was the day that made the final blow to her already bruised outlook on life. Her husband Brad was a very busy executive. Though a loving man, he was not very expressive of his emotions, and therefore never seemed to appreciate the efforts Lisa poured into the relationship. This morning, Lisa made a tragic decision. She would leave for awhile in hopes that Brad would regain his memory of why he married her to begin with. Writing a note, she discussed all her empty feelings on paper, and then slipped it under a plate left on the counter.

When Brad came home he couldn't find Lisa. Searching around he found the note under the plate left in the kitchen. In a panic he called around, but no one he called knew she had silently slipped out to her own apartment. His stomach ached as he let the phone drop through his hands and then slowly fell along side it to the floor. In agony he wept. Myriads of thoughts tormented his mind. Why did she leave? Why couldn't we talk this out? I can change! I must change!

A few days had passed by when Brad got his first phone call from Lisa. She sounded good, said things were going well, but didn't want him knowing where she was just yet. Brad told her of his great love for her and begged her to come home, but she just couldn't. Over the next several weeks Lisa called often. The conversation always seemed to be about the same, each one expressing love, each one regretting the absence, but Lisa unwilling to come home.

Brad couldn't take it any longer and hired a private investigator who soon found her whereabouts. So Brad bought a spray of flowers, drove over to Lisa's apartment, and nervously stood outside the door. In his mind, he practiced what he would say. Would he apologize first, tell her he loved her, or ask her to come home? Gradually he lifted his hand to the door knocker, and with paralyzed-like movement quietly struck it several times against the wooden door. Lisa opened the door and Brad started to say something. But, she suddenly burst into tears and fell into his arms. "Let's go home," she managed out with an overwrought voice.

Months later, after things were starting to heal in the relationship, Brad asked Lisa a question that he had been pondering since her return. "All of those times I talked to you on the phone and asked for you to come home you refused," Brad said, "Why did you come back after I went to the apartment?" Lisa's answer is what this third thought is all about. "Before," she explained, "you were just telling me you loved me and wanted me. When you came to my apartment, you showed me!"

It is the message burned into our brains by the illustrations of Jesus: "What do you think? There was a man who had two sons. He went to the first and said, 'Son, go and work today in the vineyard.' {29} "'I will not,' he answered, but later he changed his mind and went. {30} "Then the father went to the other son and said the same thing. He answered, 'I will, sir,' but he did not go. {31} "Which of the two did what his father wanted?" "The first," they answered. Jesus said to them, "I tell you the truth, the tax collectors and the prostitutes are entering the kingdom of God ahead of you. (Mat 21:28–31 NIV).

Doing is better than saying! That's true in our relationship with God, and it's true with our relationship with others. People seem to learn more by what they watch than what they're told. In relating to his wife, children, or spiritual offspring a man is measured by his actions. His dealings will be deliberated over, and they will be remembered in honor or dishonor for many years. My father's dealings with his family are remembered honorably; I want nothing less in mine!

Hang On

In a sobering reminder Solomon instructs us that: "Fire tests the purity of silver and gold, but the LORD tests the heart." (Prov 17:3 NLT). Things of the world will test the things of the world, but only God will test the character of the human heart. A question I like to ponder on is: What kind of things has God produced in me through the crucible of life's tests? In what ways am I intimate with the world and foreign to my Creator?

The essence of this book reflects the admonition given by John: "Do not love the world or anything in the world. If anyone loves the world, the love of the Father is not in him. For everything in the world the cravings of sinful man, the lust of his eyes and the boasting of what he has and does comes not from the Father but from the world." (1 John 2:15 16 NIV). That is how one falls prey to the "lie," it is through our cravings for the "things" of this world, it is through our own lust to have all that we see within our reach, and, finally through the bragging of those things to the exclusion of God. The "lie" is made more believable because it consoles us with the idea that it's okay to have that which is offered, and credits it to God. Just as the serpent in the Garden of Eden, the "lie" has taken many down the wrong path to happiness and success in life. Never will the human soul be ultimately satisfied through the things of this world. They are the roadblocks to a true and intimate connection that bridges the heavenly within us to the heavenly One beyond.

I'm beginning to understand what Jesus meant about the poor being more fortunate in the end, and why He told the rich young man to: "…go, sell your possessions and give to the poor, and you will have treasure in heaven. Then come, follow me." (Mat 19:21 NIV). I confess that through most of my years of growing up poor it was hard to embrace the wisdom in that, but now I concede, we are not blessed by what we have, but by "What" has us.

It is the things of God that are worth holding on to. They are not easy to achieve, or glamorous, nor without sacrifice, but, they are the only way to truly experience life. The story is told of a commuter flight originating in Portland, Maine, and heading to Boston, Massachusetts. The flight path took the small commuter plane across several miles of open Ocean water. Somewhere over the Atlantic the Pilot, Henry Dempsey, heard a disturbing noise originating from the rear of the plane. Handing the controls over to his co-pilot, he stepped back to check it out. When he reached the tail section, the plane hit a bit of turbulence that threw Dempsey hard against the rear door. The door flung open, sucking him out in an instant of horror.

The co-pilot, seeing that the red light warning for the opened rear door had come on, realized that the worst had happened. He radioed to the nearest tower requesting permission to land the plane immediately. He also gave the coordinates of the plane, requesting a search over that area of ocean, in hopes to find Dempsey still alive.

When the little plane taxied in from her landing, airport authorities found Dempsey hanging on to the outside ladder of the plane. He had hung on for ten minutes, at a speed that reached 200 miles per hour, and landed with his head just a few inches from hitting the runway. It took the airport personnel several minutes to pry his fingers off the ladder.[54]

Hanging on to the things of God is tough, turbulence is everywhere in the world, but, the alternatives are not good either. You can't let go! When they truly consider their choices, the people with wisdom look for the "road less traveled." One day I'll meet up with my father again, in a place of economic and social equality. I would like to thank him for the example he left myself and others. I would like to congratulate him for his steady hand at the "wheel" of life. I look forward to introducing him to his legacy, the lives of my children, and their children after them. Thanks dad, from the bottom of my heart.

> This Life's dim Windows of the Soul
> Distort the Heavens from Pole to Pole.
> And lead you to Believe a Lie
> When you see with not thro the Eye.[55]

Conclusion

Small Group Discussion Questions
End Review

1. Name some choices you've made that have proven to be life changers.

2. Does life seem to be more complicated now than it was fifty years ago? Based on your answer, how does that affect your spiritual choices?

3. "You will be yoked to something. You have no choice about enslavement, but you can choose what you want to be enslaved by." In what ways does freedom in the world enslave you and enslavement to Christ free you?

4. Have you ever practiced "fox hole" religion? What does God say about keeping our vows? [cf. Nu 30.2; Deut 23.21–23; Eccles 5.4–5; Mt 5.36–37; Jms 5.12]

5. Why is this being referred to as the "culture of violence?" Do you agree?

6. Have you ever gotten something you craved after and credited it to God's provision?

Final Exercise

1. On four index cards, writing down one thing per card, note the four most important things in your life. Look them over and eliminate two of the least important cards, one at a time. Holding in your hand the cards representing the two most important things in your life, narrow them down to just one. Is the card you are left with something that you can live without?

2. If you've been honest in answering the review questions, you probably have concluded to adjust at least one thing in your life. What will that be? Are you willing to be accountable for doing that?

3. Think of the one thing in the book that you had the most issue with when you initially read it. Read that section again to see if you still have the same degree of concern with it.

4. As you read the book, perhaps you've reflected on what you would want to be remembered for. Take the time to discuss that with the Creator.

5. What are you passionate about that would make a positive change in either the life of society or an individual, but nobody else seems to be feeling, seeing, or hearing it? Could God be asking you to get it started? Again, take the time to discuss that with Him.

6. Determine to live as if this place is not your home, to act as one respecting a moral Creator, to understand your purpose and value to Him, and to seek ways of "passing down a legacy."

Endnotes

Chapter 1: Growing Up Poor

1   [BusinessWeek "Earthly Empires" May 23, 2005 p.87]

Chapter 2: Being Satisfied in a Land of Plenty

2   I Will Lift My Eyes, Written by Bebo Norman, CM Lyrics:
    http://www.circularmoney.com/lyrics/4/bniwlme.html

3   [1/28/03 address]

4   [Business Week, May 23, 2005, Managing The Mega Church,
    p. 86]

5   Strong's Exhaustive Concordance–Crusade Bible Publishers,
    Inc.—Word reference #3772

6   Strong's Exhaustive Concordance #3107

7   Strong's Exhaustive Concordance #2129

Chapter 3: Dissatisfaction Leads To Discouragement

8   http://www.newstepsolutions.com/debt-statistics.htm
    November 3, 2006

9   Interview by Diane Sawyer with Franklin Graham, Good
    Morning America, September 16, 2005

10 [Katharina von Schlegel: "Be Still My Soul"–The New Church
    Hymnal 1976 #370]

Chapter 4: The Content and the Cravers—
The Haves and the Have Nots

11 [Famous Money Quotes from http://www.basicquotations.
com/index.php?cid=75 November 3, 2006]

Preface to Lie #2

12 Newsweek September 5,2005 Special Report: Spirituality
2005 In Search of The Spiritual pp. 48–49

13 Ibid p. 49

14 http://www.barna.org/FlexPageaspx?Page=BarnaUpdate&B
arnaUpdateID=170

November 04,2006 The Barna Group, Ltd., 1957 Eastman
Ave. Ste B, Ventura, California 93003

Chapter 5: Brittle Standards

15 "My Spiritual Journey"–An excerpt from "The Audacity of
Hope" by Barack Obama

In Time Magazine p. 60—October 23, 2006

16 "My Spiritual Journey"–An excerpt from "The Audacity of
Hope" by Barack Obama

In Time Magazine p. 60–October 23, 2006

17 The Miraculous Human Body, Citation: Jeff Arthurs references
Dr. John Medina, genetic engineer, University of Washington,
in 1995 lecture at Multnomah Bible College, Portland, Oregon
[http://www.sermoncentral.com/illustration]

Chapter 6: Our Source of Life

18 The New Century Dictionary, D. Appleton-Century Company, New York and London, Vol. 1, 1927

Preface to Lie #3

19 U.S. Census Bureau–U.S. and World Population Clocks–POPClocks

http://www.census.gov/main/www/popclock.html

Chapter 8: Metamorphosis

20 Quickverse for Windows version 4.0f–Craig Rairdin and Parsons Technology

Strong's Exhaustive Concordance–Crusade Bible Publishers, Inc.—Word reference #4964

21 Quickverse for Windows version 4.0f–Craig Rairdin and Parsons Technology

Strong's Exhaustive Concordance–Crusade Bible Publishers, Inc.—Word reference #3339

22 The City Naturalist - Monarch Butterfly—http://www.nysite.com/nature/fauna/monar.htm

23 An Introduction to Insect Life Changes—http://www.earth-life.net/insects/lifecycles.html—Metamorphosis

24 Quickverse for Windows version 4.0f–Craig Rairdin and Parsons Technology

Strong's Exhaustive Concordance–Crusade Bible Publishers, Inc.—Word reference #342

25 Transformed–Written by Mrs. F.G. Burroughs, 20th Century–The Advent Christian Hymnal, 1976, p. 355

Chapter 9: God Heals The Desperate

26 Tripod webpage–The Little Girl and Pearl Necklace—http://members.tripod.com/vitamvas/littlegirl.html

Chapter 10: Big Rocks

27 Big Rocks: A Marketing Cooperative—http://www.big-rocks.net/

28 About: Quotations—Albert Einstein, Value Quotes, from Simran Khurana http://quotations.about.com/cs/inspiration-quotes/a/Value2.htm

Preface to Lie #4

29 "Rolling Stone"–September 3, 1981 by Dave Marsh–Harry Chapin 1942–1981

30 "Cats In The Cradle" by Harry and Sandy Chapin–http://www.harrychapin.com/music/cats.shtml

31 "Feminism"Wikipedia—http://en.wikipedia.org/wiki/Feminism

32 "Feminist theory"–Radical Feminism—Wikipedia—http://en.wikipedia.org/wiki/Feminist_theory

33 "The Agony of Feminism: Why Feminist Theory Is Necessary After All"—Nina Baym http://bailiwick.lib.uiowa.edu/wstudies/theory.html—Originally published in *The Emperor ReDressed: Critiquing Critical Theory*, ed Dwight Eddins. Tuscaloosa: UNIversity of Alabama Press, 1995, pp. 101-117.—http://www.english.uiuc.edu/-people-/emeritus/baym/essays/feminism.htm

34 Poem by Will Allen Dromgoole, StoryBin.com http://www.storybin.com/builders/builders165.shtml

Chapter 11: The Rogue Elephants

35 See also BBC News article for February 14, 2000–"Elephants Kill Endangered Rhino" http://news.bbc.co.uk/2/hi/africa/642731.stm

36 The Robesonian Online, Violent Streak: County sees upsurge of teenage mayhem— http://www.robesonian.com/

Monday, October 30, 2006 By Matt Elofson and Jonathan Yeomans - Staff writers

37 The New Century Dictionary, p. 840

38 Joe Paterno from About Quotations–Simran Khurana http://quotations.about.com/cs/inspiration-quotes/a/Integrity7.htm?terms=quote+by%20joe%20paterno

Chapter 12: Will You Take This Woman?

39 Greek-English Dictionary of the New Testament by Barclay M. Newman, Jr. United Bible Societies, London 1971 p. 48

40 Strong's Exhaustive Concordance–Crusade Bible Publishers, Inc.—Word reference p.126 #8669

41 Strong's Exhaustive Concordance–Crusade Bible Publishers, Inc.—Word reference p.74 #4910

42 Quickverse for Windows version 4.0f–Craig Rairdin and Parsons Technology

Strong's Exhaustive Concordance–Crusade Bible Publishers, Inc.—Word reference #5259

43 Quickverse for Windows version 4.0f–Craig Rairdin and Parsons Technology

Strong's Exhaustive Concordance–Crusade Bible Publishers, Inc.—Word reference #5021

44 "Wind Beneath My Wings" [quotes], Bette Midler, The lyric archive—http://www.thelyricarchive.com/index.shtml

45 Covenant: BibleGateway.com–1995–2006–Easton's 1897 Bible Dictionary http://www.biblegateway.com/resources/dictionaries/dict_meaning.php?source=1&wid=T0000916

46 cf. Genesis 15:5–18

47 An Historical Survey of the Old Testament, Eugene H. Merrill, 1966 The Craig Press, Nutley, New Jersey p. 76

Chapter 13: Sorry About Wendy's

48 New Century Dictionary D. Appleton-Century Company, New York, 1927 p. 89

49 Meltdown at Augusta, Rick Reilly, Sports Illustrated 12/30/96–01/06/97, Vol. 85 Issue 27, p. 66, 2p, 1c

50 Meltdown at Augusta, Rick Reilly, Sports Illustrated 12/30/96–01/06/97, Vol. 85 Issue 27, p. 66

Conclusion

51 The Road Not Taken, Robert Frost, Complete Poems of Robert Frost, 1949, 131

52 Freedom, Love, and Forgiveness, Promise of Love, 1995 T.K. Ministries, Inc., by Questar, Inc. Written by   M i c h a e l Cody–Used by permission

53 Julius Caesar, Act I, Scene 2 pp. 140–141—http://www.enotes.com/jc-text/3481#thefault

R.   Moore. "Shakespeare Quotes's Famous Quotations— Enotes.com LLC, October 2001. 3 November 2006

54 Perseverance—Illustrations For Preaching and Teaching–
    Editor Craig Brian Larson, Baker, p.114

    http://www.biblecenter.com/illustrations/perseverance.htm

55 William Blake, "The Everlasting Gospel," The Poetry and
    Prose of William Blake, ed. David V. Erdman {Garden City,
    N.Y.: Doubleday & Company, Inc. Copyright by David V.
    Erdman and Harold Sloan, 1965}, p. 512, 1.100–104